MUSIC COVER LESSONS

Helen Tierney

First published 2012 in Great Britain by Rhinegold Education, 14-15 Berners Street, London W1T 3LJ, UK
www.rhinegoldeducation.co.uk

© 2012 Rhinegold Education, a division of Music Sales Limited

All rights reserved. The worksheets and factsheets can be photocopied for educational use. Otherwise no part of this publication may be reproduced, stored in a retrieval system, or transmitted in any form or by any means, electronic, mechanical, photocopying, recording or otherwise, without the prior permission of Rhinegold Education.

Music Cover Lessons • Order No. RHG435 • ISBN: 978-1-78038-606-5

Exclusive Distributors: Music Sales Ltd, Distribution Centre, Newmarket Road, Bury St Edmunds, Suffolk IP33 3YB, UK

Printed in the EU

All images courtesy of Corbis, Getty Images and iStock.

Exodus. Words & Music by Bob Marley. © Copyright 1977 Fifty-Six Hope Road Music Limited/Blackwell Fuller Music Publishing LLC. Administered by Blue Mountain Music Limited. All Rights Reserved. International Copyright Secured.

One Love. Words & Music by Bob Marley. © Copyright 1977 Fifty-Six Hope Road Music Limited/Blackwell Fuller Music Publishing LLC. Administered by Blue Mountain Music Limited. All Rights Reserved. International Copyright Secured.

Extract from Mandela, N., *Long Walk to Freedom*, published by Little Brown & Co. (1994).

www.rhinegoldeducation.co.uk

CONTENTS

Introduction	3
Medieval music	5
Baroque music	11
Classical music	17
Romantic music	23
Jazz	29
Blues	35
British folk music	41
Reggae	47
African music	53
Indian music	59

CD-ROM contents

The CD-ROM includes ten PowerPoint presentations that accompany each of the topics in this book. These presentations include:

- A reduction of the information in the factsheets and worksheets
- Colour images to accompany the facts and activities
- Links to the YouTube playlists that have been created for each topic, providing you with a quick way to access relevant listening examples.

PDFs of all the factsheets and worksheets are also included on the CD-ROM, allowing you to print these out instead of photocopying them if you wish. In addition, two detailed lesson plans are given on the CD-ROM which you can use as templates to create your own.

INTRODUCTION

This resource is a response to the problem of music cover work.

Too often, work set for music cover lessons seems irrelevant or disjointed from both everyday learning and the skills on which students need to focus in KS3 and KS4 music curricula. *Music Cover Lessons* provides a solution through ten learning experiences based around stylistic awareness, an understanding of key terms and an appreciation of musical traditions.

The main aim of every music lesson should be to enable students to experience music and use it as the fundamental language of learning. However, this is often not possible for covering staff. The regular music teacher may be the only music specialist in the school. Cover teachers may have little or no contact with either the music staff or the department's ethos and may have little knowledge of the musical abilities of the students. This resource takes that emergency absence and the need for useful and relevant work as its starting point.

A valuable learning experience

Music Cover Lessons builds on written activities with add-on practical tasks and listening links. It emphasises key words and basic features of musical styles, and introduces social and cultural contexts. Activities take different learning styles into account and there are simpler tasks as well as higher-level questions.

Designed to work in the worst-case scenario of a non-specialist room with no audio or internet facilities, *Music Cover Lessons* provides enough content, reading and absorption of key terms and features on its factsheets to make lessons valuable learning experiences, even if music cannot be played. Basic activities can subsequently be broadened through the addition of audio extracts, and practical exploration of each style is kept deliberately simple for the non-specialist covering teacher to deliver. Some teachers may be able to play a more active part in delivering key content and discussion, while others may wish students to work through the activities individually and in their own chosen way.

Multi-purpose

The lessons will also work well as GCSE revision, Year 9 bridging or simply as a standard KS3 initial lesson or refresher session. The ten topics have been chosen for their common coverage at both key stages, and the activities have sufficient detail for a mainstream KS4 lesson as well as KS3. In addition, most GCSE specifications cover many of the chosen styles, and the lessons can be used either as introductions or revision sessions. With the additional optional practical tasks, the ten lessons can easily be extended into 20 to cover longer-term absence or to support regular lessons.

Flexibility designed for the non-specialist

The activities for each topic are set out with flexibility and choice in mind, for both teacher and students:

- Activities feature content for students with different learning styles and include simpler tasks as well as higher-level questions.
- Practical tasks are designed for the non-specialist to deliver if they feel confident for the class to work through them.
- Suggested lesson outlines take students' prior knowledge into account. The teacher can then decide which route to follow: using all of the written and listening tasks, individual or paired work, mixing practical with written tasks or working through a sequence as a whole class.

- The PowerPoint presentations on the CD-ROM provide a reduction of the information in the factsheets and worksheets, enhanced with colour images.
- All of the suggested listening extracts have been collated into YouTube playlists for easy access, which are linked to from the PowerPoint presentations. These extracts can provide a stimulating audio backdrop to activities and written tasks, as well as providing starting points for discussion as students learn about the relevant style.

Whether you are a professional cover teacher, a harassed head of expressive arts having to provide last-minute cover for an absentee teacher, a music teacher swamped by concert rehearsals with four cover lessons to set in non-specialist rooms the next day, or simply a teacher who needs a solid guide to these very teachable topics, *Music Cover Lessons* will provide accessible and easy-to-deliver solutions.

Photocopiable and printable handouts

All of the factsheets and worksheets in this book can be photocopied for educational use. PDFs of the student handouts are also provided on the CD-ROM, allowing you to print rather than photocopy them if you wish.

Relevance to KS3 and KS4

Music Cover Lessons is designed specifically to provide lessons based around the most commonly studied musical styles covered by KS3 courses and GCSE specifications. These include Western classical traditions (medieval, Baroque, Classical and Romantic), world music (Indian, African, reggae and British folk), and jazz and blues. Within this stylistic range, all music departments should be able to find a use for many of the mixed-ability activities and topics presented in this resource, whether at KS3 or KS4.

Following the guidance of the National Curriculum, the importance of how music reflects time, place and culture forms the basis of these lessons. For KS3, links to other subjects such as Religious Studies, History, PSHE and Geography can also reinforce the cross-curricular studies and connections encouraged by all schools.

All of the GCSE specifications make reference to many of the musical traditions covered here. This can make *Music Cover Lessons* ideal for teachers needing either KS4 revision resources or one-off introductory lessons to a particular style.

About the author

Helen Tierney was born in Merseyside and studied music at Oxford University. She has taught music in comprehensive schools for over 20 years and currently works at Queen Elizabeth's Girls' School in Barnet, where she is also AST for secondary music. She has also worked with music in prisons, dementia units and eating disorders clinics. She currently examines for the ABRSM and sings with the BBC Symphony Chorus.

TEACHER'S NOTES

MEDIEVAL MUSIC

EQUIPMENT REQUIRED

- Copies of the Factsheet to be handed out to students.
- Copies of the Written Activities worksheet to be handed out to students.
- Paper or exercise books to complete written work.
- Copies of the Practical Activities worksheet, if you feel confident in allowing students to undertake these tasks. The practical activities will require instruments (ideally keyboards or music ICT) for students to work on. Tuned percussion, guitars or the students' own instruments can also be used.
- An interactive whiteboard (optional). A PowerPoint presentation that accompanies this topic is available on the CD-ROM. This includes a reduction of the information on the factsheet and worksheets, accompanied by colour images. It also includes a link to the YouTube playlist for this topic (see below).

SUGGESTED LISTENING EXTRACTS

The following extracts are available in the YouTube playlist for this topic, which can be accessed from the PowerPoint presentation on the CD-ROM or from Rhinegold Education's YouTube channel.

- **Early Music Consort: a medieval concert**
- **Dufay Collective:** *Saltarello*
- **Hurdy gurdy demonstration**
- **Psaltery demonstration**
- **Shawm demonstration**
- **An example of plainchant**
- **An example of organum**
- **Lumina Vocal Ensemble:** *Summer is Icumen In*

Teachers may wish to use the Early Music Consort or Dufay Collective extracts as a starting point, either as students enter the room or as a starting activity, for students to pool or mindmap their prior knowledge of medieval music. Reference is made in the Factsheet to the Dufay Collective, and the class could discuss and offer their views on why medieval music is still performed today, either as an initial activity or as a plenary discussion.

PRIOR KNOWLEDGE

The Factsheet provides the basic grounding in this subject that is required at both KS3 and KS4. No prior knowledge is needed from students. However, pointing out links to History (many Year 7 students study medieval topics, especially the Battle of Hastings) and any study of Chaucer in English will help students to get a sense of period and time.

SUGGESTED LESSON OUTLINE

A YouTube playlist is available that contains the suggested listening extracts listed on the left. It is not essential, but it is useful to have extracts playing while the students are working.

A suggested starting activity would be to play an extract and ask the class to pool their knowledge and/or views on the musical style before giving out the Factsheet. If the cover work is being set as a revision exercise on a previously studied topic, this will be particularly valuable.

The Factsheet contains all of the information needed to complete the activities. You may wish students to read through it individually, or in pairs or small groups. The Activities worksheets can be given out with the Factsheet or afterwards. The activities can be undertaken in any order, and some students may wish to focus on a particular one or two.

If you feel confident with both the practical and written activities, you may wish to mix and match the tasks within a lesson. The material can also be split across two lessons, with the first lesson focusing on going over the Factsheet and completing the written work, and the second lesson based on the practical tasks.

Alternatively, completing two written tasks and starting off the practical work can fit within an hour-long lesson. The tasks could be completed in the next session if desired by the returning subject teacher (or the cover teacher if required).

TEACHER'S NOTES

MEDIEVAL MUSIC

SUGGESTED LISTENING EXTRACTS (cont.)

If you are planning to read through the Factsheet as a class rather than individually, you may wish to break up the text with clips of the performances, particularly the hurdy gurdy, the medieval concert and the Dufay Collective *Saltarello*, and ask students to pick out instruments they can recognise using the Factsheet.

SUGGESTED LESSON OUTLINE (cont.)

Plenary activities can focus on key word terminology and awareness of style. Asking students to prepare three questions about the style and getting them to quiz each other is a simple follow-on activity, as is asking the class to list as many key words linked to the topic as possible without using their Factsheets.

If practical work is not an option, breaking up the written work with audio or visual clips of performances will ensure that the class receives a solid experience of the style.

FACTSHEET

MEDIEVAL MUSIC

INTRODUCTION

Historians usually think of medieval times as AD 500 to 1400. Just imagine how different music was in those days compared to now – for example, think about what it would be like if the only time you ever heard music was when it was played live. This Factsheet will give you some basic information about medieval music that will help you to complete the Activities worksheets.

> **YOU ONLY EVER HEARD MUSIC IN MEDIEVAL TIMES WHEN IT WAS PLAYED LIVE!**

INSTRUMENTS

Medieval instruments were largely made out of wood and animal materials such as gut and skin, which rot away over time. This means that most instruments from that period no longer exist. We have to rely on images from paintings and evidence such as carvings or stained glass pictures of angels in medieval churches to know what instruments were like in those days.

Medieval stained glass window showing an angel with a lute

There were no orchestras in medieval times. Instead, bands would have been put together with whatever instruments were available. Sometimes they are classified into two groups: outdoors (loud instruments such as trumpet, drum, bagpipes) and indoors (quiet instruments such as psaltery, harp and fiddle).

You will see that some of these instruments have very similar descendents in the orchestra today, while others no longer have a place. However, all of them are still being made as reproductions and played by musicians specialising in medieval (also known as early) music. One such band doing this is the Dufay Collective.

HURDY GURDY
A stringed instrument played by turning the handle. It has a built-in **drone**.

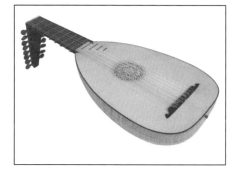

LUTE A stringed instrument similar to the guitar.

HARP
Much smaller than the modern version in the orchestra.

PSALTERY
A string instrument with a sound-board. Strings could be plucked with quills or by hand.

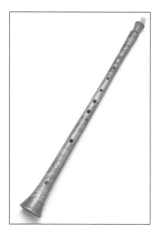

SHAWM
An ancestor of the oboe.

Drone: repeated or sustained notes played to accompany melodies.

FACTSHEET

MEDIEVAL MUSIC

FEATURES OF MEDIEVAL MUSIC

Medieval music did not use major or minor scales. Instead there were **modes**: scales that can be played nowadays on the white notes of a piano. These scales still survive today and are often used in styles of music such as jazz and folk. Two common modes used in medieval music are the Aeolian mode and Dorian mode:

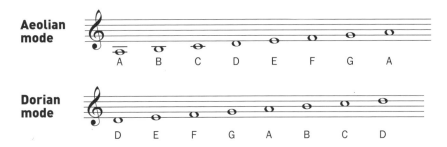

Medieval music also used **drones**, which are repeated or sustained notes played to accompany melodies. Drones could often be two notes played together, such as D and A: an interval of a 5th (five notes apart).

WHO PLAYED AND SANG MEDIEVAL MUSIC?

We can divide medieval music into two categories:

Sacred

This refers to religious music. The Christian Church developed styles such as **plainchant** and, later, **polyphonic** music. Starting with just a single melody line, chant then developed further, with musicians starting to add a sense of harmony (notes played or sung together). An example of this is **organum**, where another vocal part is added to the basic chant melody. The additional vocal part is often a 4th or 5th below the melody line.

> **Plainchant:** religious words sung in Latin to a single melody line.

> **Polyphonic music:** pieces with two or more independent parts, often written for choirs. One type of polyphonic music is the motet.

Monks worked on developing ways of writing music down that were in some ways quite similar to modern notation. Often these manuscripts were beautifully illustrated (we call these 'illuminated') and many are now displayed in museums and cathedrals.

Secular

This is the term we give to non-religious music, such as drinking songs, dances, love songs and ballads (songs that tell a story). People who performed these were like our modern-day buskers. Most travelled around performing in villages and towns, and were known as **minstrels** (in England), **troubadours** (in France) and **minnesingers** (in Germany).

Although some pieces were written down, most musicians learned by listening and copying, which we call an **oral tradition**. Secular songs were often about love and chivalry, but they also recounted tales of distant lands and historical events.

Although people in medieval times knew a lot of music, most did not hear new pieces and sounds very often. This only happened when groups of travelling musicians visited and brought new songs into a community. Imagine the excitement of hearing new instruments and tunes for the first time. Can you imagine not being able to access new songs via the internet and radio, and having to listen to the same playlist all the time?

MUSIC COVER LESSONS

WRITTEN ACTIVITIES

MEDIEVAL MUSIC

1 Medieval music key words

Make a list of 20 key terms linked to the theme of medieval music. Create a spider diagram to show how these words are connected and, if you have time, create a colourful border like the one in the manuscript on the Factsheet.

Here are some words to get you started:

**DRONE   MODE   HARP
PLAINCHANT   AEOLIAN**

2 Thinking about life in medieval times

How different was a medieval person's experience of music compared to yours? Think about this carefully – you may wish to discuss it with a partner and then draw up a list of similarities and differences. Take into account how we hear music played and sung, and where and when this happens. When in your daily life do you hear music? Now, in your imagination, go back to the 1200s. How would it be different?

Set out the similarities and differences in two columns.

3 A medieval diary

Imagine you were watching a medieval performance. Choose a date in medieval times and a place, and write a diary entry describing the performance. Put in as much detail as you can: what were the musicians wearing? What instruments were they playing and what did they sound like? Was there dancing? For what occasion did the musicians come to your town or village to perform? If you have time you could illustrate your account.

4 Design a true or false quiz

Using the information on the Factsheet create ten statements about medieval music – a mix of true and false. Write them out with the answers given at the end. They can be on any aspect of this style of music, such as the historical dates, instruments, features of the music or notation.

When you have finished, test a friend's knowledge by asking them to say which of your statements are true and which are false.

PRACTICAL ACTIVITIES

MEDIEVAL MUSIC

1 Using modes

Play through the Dorian mode on an instrument. On the piano, this means playing a scale that starts on D and just uses the white notes:

D E F G A B C D

Now try developing some short patterns in a lively rhythmic style suitable for a medieval dance tune. If you use a keyboard or a piano, add a drone of D and A in your left hand (at the lower end of the keyboard). Starting and finishing the melody line on a D or an A will help to establish the Dorian mode.

Once you have some basic ideas, try writing them down, either with traditional notation or using a system of your own such as letter names.

If you feel confident with what you have written, develop your ideas further by adding a percussion instrument, or using harmony (just like the organum mentioned in the Factsheet) that uses intervals of 4ths and 5ths.

2 Writing medieval song lyrics

Many medieval songs were written about the seasons – especially winter and spring as they had such a big impact on the lives of people back then.

Choose one of these seasons and write lyrics about life in medieval times in spring or winter.

Just as now, song lyrics in medieval times were often very repetitive – it's fine to use the same lines twice, for example. Once you have a verse or two, try writing a melody to your lyrics that uses the Aeolian mode. Remember, this is a scale that starts on A and uses the white notes of the piano:

You may wish to accompany your song in a medieval style with a drone on the notes A and E.

A B C D E F G A

10 MUSIC COVER LESSONS

TEACHER'S NOTES

EQUIPMENT REQUIRED

- Copies of the Factsheet to be handed out to students.
- Copies of the Written Activities worksheet to be handed out to students.
- Paper or exercise books to complete written work.
- Copies of the Practical Activities worksheet, if you feel confident in allowing students to undertake these tasks. The practical activities will require instruments (ideally keyboards or music ICT) for students to work on. Tuned percussion, guitars or the students' own instruments can also be used.
- An interactive whiteboard (optional). A PowerPoint presentation that accompanies this topic is available on the CD-ROM. This includes a reduction of the information on the factsheet and worksheets, accompanied by colour images. It also includes a link to the YouTube playlist for this topic (see below).

SUGGESTED LISTENING EXTRACTS

The following extracts are available in the YouTube playlist for this topic, which can be accessed from the PowerPoint presentation on the CD-ROM or from Rhinegold Education's YouTube channel.

- **Handel: 'Hallelujah' from *Messiah***
- **Handel: 'Hallelujah' flashmob**
- **Pachelbel: Canon in D**
- **Coolio: *C U When U Get There***
- **Vivaldi: 'Winter' Concerto**
- **Bach: Brandenburg Concerto No. 3**
- **Bach: Partita for Solo Violin No. 2**

The 'Hallelujah' chorus, either in the traditional performance or the flashmob version, may prove a lively and powerful starting point because it is such a familiar piece. The flashmob version may generate discussion on why they chose to perform that particular piece, and how well it works in the unusual modern setting.

BAROQUE MUSIC

PRIOR KNOWLEDGE

Playing students some of the famous Baroque pieces in the YouTube playlist will be a good way to introduce this topic. Students may wish to comment on the fact they have heard some of these pieces before, especially the 'Hallelujah' chorus. Changes to orchestral instruments can be another good starting point: for example, questions about string and woodwind instruments can lead on to discussions of how the orchestra has changed.

Students should also be encouraged to make links with art or literature that they have studied from this period, and instrumentalists may be able to talk about or even demonstrate pieces from the period if they are able to make connections with their own repertoire.

SUGGESTED LESSON OUTLINE

A YouTube playlist is available that contains the suggested listening extracts listed on the left. It is not essential, but it is useful to have extracts playing while the students are working.

A suggested starting activity is to play an extract and ask the class to pool their knowledge and/or views on the musical style before giving out the Factsheet. The 'Hallelujah' chorus flashmob video is an excellent starting point and can be contrasted with the more formal performance of this familiar piece. In addition, Coolio's sampling of the Pachelbel Canon is an accessible introduction to this famous piece.

You may wish students to read through the Factsheet – which contains all of the information needed to complete the tasks – individually or in pairs or small groups. The Activities worksheets can be given out with the Factsheet or afterwards. The activities can be undertaken in any order, and some students may wish to focus on a particular one or two.

TEACHER'S NOTES

SUGGESTED LISTENING EXTRACTS (cont.)

The Vivaldi 'Winter' Concerto, known to many students through its use in TV and film, is a great advertisement for the catchy nature of Baroque music, with its repeated patterns and driving rhythms. Good parallels can be made here with pop and rock.

Instrumentation can be explored through the Bach extracts, which will also help to illustrate the musical features described on the Factsheet.

ACTIVITY ANSWERS

Activity 3: the Baroque orchestra

Strings	Woodwind	Brass	Percussion	Keyboard
Violin	Oboe	Trumpet	Drums/timpani	Organ
Viola	Flute			Harpsichord
Cello	Recorder			
Bass	Bassoon			

BAROQUE MUSIC

SUGGESTED LESSON OUTLINE (cont.)

If you feel confident with both the written and practical activities, you may wish to mix and match the tasks within a lesson. The material can also be split across two lessons, with the first lesson focusing on going over the Factsheet and completing the written work, and the second lesson based on the practical tasks.

Alternatively, completing two written tasks and starting off the practical work can fit within an hour-long lesson. The tasks could be completed in the next session if desired by the returning subject teacher (or the cover teacher if required).

Plenary activities can focus on key word terminology and awareness of style. Asking students to prepare three questions about the style and getting them to quiz each other is a simple follow-on activity, as is asking the class to list as many key words linked to the topic as possible without using their Factsheets.

If practical work is not an option, breaking up the written work with audio or visual clips of performances will ensure that the class receives a solid experience of the style.

FACTSHEET

BAROQUE MUSIC

INTRODUCTION

The Baroque period lasted roughly from 1600 to 1750. Music in this era was highly ornate and often sounds very grand to us today. It used lots of fast repeated patterns and ornaments. The orchestra was based around the string section but woodwind and brass were sometimes also used, and the harpsichord and organ were the main keyboard instruments.

> **❝ BAROQUE MUSIC IS POPULAR FOR ITS STRONG SENSE OF BEAT AND LIVELY STRING WRITING, AND HAS BEEN USED IN MANY TV ADVERTS AND FILMS. ❞**

INSTRUMENTS

The Baroque orchestra was built around the string section: violins, violas, cellos and double bass. A **continuo** instrument, often the harpsichord, also played with the orchestra to strengthen the sound. Flutes or recorders, oboes, bassoons, trumpets and drums (usually timpani) were also used. Instruments such as the French horn and the clarinet had not yet been established as orchestral instruments in this period.

Baroque harpsichord

Continuo (also known as basso continuo) is the name given to the bass line instrument (such as the cello) and the instruments that played the chords (usually the harpsichord or organ). The continuo strengthened the sound of Baroque music.

FEATURES OF BAROQUE STYLE

- Trills and other **ornaments** were used to decorate melodic lines.
- Sequences of patterns moving up and down were common.
- Pieces of music usually kept to the same mood throughout.
- **Polyphonic** textures were common.
- Changes in volume tended to happen suddenly.
- The orchestra was limited in size.
- The system of having major and minor keys was established.
- Popular pieces included operas, oratorios, suites, concertos and Masses.

Ornament: a decoration in the music such as a trill or a mordent. Usually short quick patterns or added notes.

THREE FAMOUS BAROQUE COMPOSERS

	Bach	Handel	Vivaldi
Born	1685	1685	1678
Died	1750	1759	1741
Famous works	Brandenburg Concertos	Messiah	*The Four Seasons*
Life	Two wives and many children!	No wife or family	He was a Catholic priest
Location	Lived in Germany	Born in Germany, settled in London	Lived in Italy

FACTSHEET

BAROQUE MUSIC

BAROQUE KEY WORDS

Trill	An ornament played by repeatedly alternating one note quickly with another one.
Polyphonic	A type of texture where two or more independent lines are played together.
Harpsichord	An ancestor of the piano with strings inside that are plucked, not struck.
Ternary form	A piece with three sections, where the two outer sections are the same and the middle one is different (ABA).
Fugue	A polyphonic piece where the musical lines imitate each other.
Aria	A solo song in an opera or oratorio.
Oratorio	A religious work similar to an opera but not acted out.
Concerto	A piece for solo instrument and orchestra.
Binary form	A piece with two contrasting sections (AB).

BAROQUE COMPOSERS

Baroque composers could not always choose to write what they wanted to in the way that composers can today. They often earned money writing religious or sacred music. For example, Bach produced music each week for Sunday church services in Germany. Composers also made a living writing operas, which became hugely popular in Baroque times, and Handel was a prominent composer in this field. Courts and royal figures would employ composers – Pachelbel, for example, worked at various royal courts in Germany as an organist as well as carrying out other musical duties. As such, composers in Baroque times were dependent on the Church, courts, royal individuals and theatres to make a living.

THREE FAMOUS BAROQUE PIECES

1. The 'Hallelujah' chorus from Handel's *Messiah* (1741)

One of the most popular pieces for choir ever written, this is a chorus from *Messiah*, which is an **oratorio**. It is written for four types of voice: soprano, alto, tenor and bass. The choir and orchestra combined produce an uplifting sound. The piece was famously used in a shopping mall in the USA in a 'flashmob' activity that became an internet sensation. Check it out!

2. Pachelbel's Canon, composed in the 1690s

A canon is a piece of music that is **polyphonic**. One part copies another but is slightly delayed. Pachelbel's Canon is built over a repeated chord pattern that continues all the way through. It has inspired other musicians to create their own similar pieces, including the rap artist Coolio in his 1997 hit *C U When U Get There*.

3. *The Four Seasons* by Vivaldi (1725)

This is a set of four concertos (pieces for solo violin and orchestra). Each season is described musically. We call this kind of descriptive music **programme music**. These pieces are popular for their strong sense of beat and lively string writing, and have been used in many TV adverts and films.

Coolio

Programme music: instrumental music that has been written to describe images, scenes, stories or events.

MUSIC COVER LESSONS

WRITTEN ACTIVITIES

BAROQUE MUSIC

1. Baroque key words

Using at least 20 key words about Baroque music, make a spider diagram in your book or on a piece of paper to show how the terms are related. Include composer names and facts about them, instruments, and words to describe the Baroque style.

2. Baroque composers

What would it be like to be a Baroque composer living and composing in the 1700s?

Make a list of six differences that describe how a Baroque composer might work compared to one today. Think about how we listen to music, how music is performed and how you can write it down. Can you think of some things that all composers – whether living today or in Baroque times – have to deal with?

Winter scene

4. Design an album cover or poster

Whenever polls are taken of people's favourite classical pieces, Vivaldi's *Four Seasons* is always in the top ten and it is performed regularly around the world. 'Winter' is the most popular concerto of the four.

Design your own album cover or poster for a live performance of this work. Choose a venue, either a local one or a famous venue such as the Royal Albert Hall. Make sure the composer's name and title of the piece are clearly shown. You may wish to draw inspiration from the image to the left, and listen to the music if possible. What does it make you feel? What images does it bring to mind?

3. The Baroque orchestra

Using the information about the Baroque orchestra on your Factsheet, draw up a list of the different instruments used at that time in their orchestral families. You can use the format of the table below – some answers have been added to get you started. You could also include a list of instruments used now that were not used in Baroque orchestras. Why was this?

Strings	Woodwind	Brass	Percussion	Keyboard
Violin	Oboe			Organ

BAROQUE MUSIC 15

PRACTICAL ACTIVITIES

BAROQUE MUSIC

1 Composing a Baroque ground bass

For this activity you are going to devise a repeated bass line and add a melody on top, just like in Pachelbel's Canon. Either use one of the bass lines given below, or make up you own. If you are composing your own, make sure the bass line uses steady slow notes and is not too complicated.

Here is a simple bass line with just four long notes:

C G F G

This bass line has slightly more variety in rhythm:

C B A F G C B A F G

Practise playing your bass line, repeating it over and over again without any pauses to create a 'ground bass', just like the one in Pachelbel's Canon.

Now, using the notes of the key you have chosen for your bass line (such as all the white notes for a bass line in C major), make up your own melodies to go over the top. Try to make the tune build up and get more complex as it goes on. Then individually or in pairs, practise playing your bass line and tune together.

Your melody can use **scales** like this:

C D E F G A B C   C D E F G A B C

Or **sequences** like this (a sequence is a repeating pattern that moves up or down):

C B A G   B A G F   A G F E   G F E D

2 Composing wintry music

Look at the image of a winter scene on the Written Activities worksheet. Like Vivaldi, you are going to devise a short piece to describe the mood of winter.

Use the key of A minor and make use of scales and sequences. Remember, the A minor scale is:

　　A B C D E F G♯ A

The two main chords (tonic and dominant) are:

　　A C E   and   E G♯ B

Add in ornaments to the melody line and remember that music such as Vivaldi's used lots of repeats. Look at the picture carefully. What sort of tempo or speed does it suggest? Can you think of how you might show the freezing cold? Playing chords in a shimmering effect (tremolo) and using trills might help to create a wintry mood.

If possible, listen to Vivaldi's 'Winter' concerto for inspiration. You could even add contemporary beats and sounds to create a Baroque/21st century fusion.

TEACHER'S NOTES

CLASSICAL MUSIC

EQUIPMENT REQUIRED

- Copies of the Factsheet to be handed out to students.
- Copies of the Written Activities worksheet to be handed out to students.
- Paper or exercise books to complete written work.
- Copies of the Practical Activities worksheet, if you feel confident in allowing students to undertake these tasks. The practical activities will require instruments (ideally keyboards or music ICT) for students to work on. Tuned percussion, guitars or the students' own instruments can also be used.
- An interactive whiteboard (optional). A PowerPoint presentation that accompanies this topic is available on the CD-ROM. This includes a reduction of the information on the factsheet and worksheets, accompanied by colour images. It also includes a link to the YouTube playlist for this topic (see below).

SUGGESTED LISTENING EXTRACTS

The following extracts are available in the YouTube playlist for this topic, which can be accessed from the PowerPoint presentation on the CD-ROM or from Rhinegold Education's YouTube channel.

- Mozart: Symphony No. 40, first movement
- Mozart: *Alla Turca* from Piano Sonata No. 11
- Mozart: *Eine Kleine Nachtmusik*
- Clips from the film *Amadeus*
- Beethoven: *Für Elise*
- Beethoven: 'Moonlight' Sonata
- Beethoven: *Ode to Joy* from Symphony No. 9
- 'Joyful joyful' from *Sister Act 2*
- Haydn: 'Farewell' Symphony, last movement
- Haydn: 'The Heavens are Telling' from *The Creation*

PRIOR KNOWLEDGE

Students do not need any prior knowledge of the period and the activities can be set as an introductory or one-off lesson. You may wish to see if students have studied any music by Mozart or Beethoven, such as piano pieces for grade exams studied in private music lessons. Students may also have studied Baroque or Romantic music, and links can be made to these in the context of understanding general musical history and development.

SUGGESTED LESSON OUTLINE

A YouTube playlist is available that contains the suggested listening extracts listed to the left. It is not essential, but it is useful to have extracts playing while the students are working.

A suggested starting activity is to play an extract from the YouTube playlist and ask the class to pool their knowledge and/or views on the musical style before giving out the Factsheet. Playing extracts such as Mozart's Symphony No. 40 or Beethoven's *Für Elise* will be a good starting point for drawing students into the topic and building on their awareness of this music. If the cover work is being set as a revision exercise on a previously studied topic, this will be particularly valuable.

You may wish students to read through the Factsheet – which contains all of the information needed to complete the tasks – individually or in pairs or small groups. The Activities worksheets can be given out with the Factsheet or afterwards.

The activities can be undertaken in any order and some students may wish to focus on a particular one or two. If you feel confident with both the written and practical activities, you may wish to mix and match the tasks within a lesson. The material can also be split across two lessons, with the first lesson focusing on going over the Factsheet and completing the written work, and the second lesson based on the practical tasks.

TEACHER'S NOTES

CLASSICAL MUSIC

SUGGESTED LISTENING EXTRACTS (cont.)

The most immediately recognisable of these extracts are probably *Für Elise*, *Alla Turca* and Mozart's Symphony No. 40. Any of these will be a good starting point for introducing the lesson content. You may wish to focus on the chronology of the composers to give a sense of progression, i.e. early Classical (Haydn), middle period (Mozart) and late Classical (Beethoven). Note that several of the extracts have been used as mobile ringtones (for example *Für Elise*, the 'Moonlight' Sonata and *Eine Kleine Nachtmusik*). This would be a good prompt for focusing on Classical melodies – their balance, shape and general catchiness.

Ode to Joy will be familiar to many students. You may wish to explore this further with the extract 'Joyful joyful' from the finale of *Sister Act 2*, which is a reworking of this piece with rap and street dance routines.

SUGGESTED LESSON OUTLINE (cont.)

Alternatively, completing two written tasks and starting off the practical work can fit within an hour-long lesson. The tasks could be completed in the next session if desired by the returning subject teacher (or the cover teacher if required).

Plenary activities can focus on key word terminology and awareness of style. Asking students to prepare three questions about the style and getting them to quiz each other is a simple follow-on activity, as is asking the class to list as many key words linked to the topic as possible without using their Factsheets.

ACTIVITY ANSWERS

Activity 1: Classical key words

a)	A piece of music for orchestra in four movements	**Symphony**
b)	The first section of sonata form	**Exposition**
c)	The type of texture most common in the Classical period	**Homophonic**
d)	The nationality of Mozart and Haydn	**Austrian**
e)	A type of chamber music using two violins, a viola and a cello	**String quartet**
f)	A piece for solo instrument and orchestra in three movements	**Concerto**
g)	The word for volume in music	**Dynamics**
h)	The composer of *The Creation*	**Haydn**
i)	The composer of *The Magic Flute*	**Mozart**
j)	An instrument added to the orchestra in the Classical period	**Clarinet**

MUSIC COVER LESSONS

FACTSHEET

CLASSICAL MUSIC

INTRODUCTION

To many people, the term 'Classical music' means music that uses an orchestra or operatic style of singing, but the term really applies to music composed approximately between 1750 and 1820. This period of Western music history follows the Baroque period (1600–1750) and comes before the Romantic period.

> **CLASSICAL MUSIC IS ABOUT BALANCE, GRACEFUL PHRASING AND REFINED TEXTURES.**

TYPES OF WORK

Composers particularly enjoyed writing the following types of work during the Classical period:

- **Opera:** a large-scale dramatic work for solo singers, orchestra and chorus.
- **Chamber music:** music for small ensembles (groups that could fit into 'chambers' or smaller rooms instead of concert halls). The string quartet is a good example of this – it consists of two violins, a viola and cello.
- **Concerto:** a piece for solo instrument and orchestra in three movements. It allows the soloist to show off their skill and virtuosity.
- **Symphony:** a piece for orchestra in four movements.

FEATURES OF CLASSICAL MUSIC

Here are some of the main features of music in the Classical style:

Larger orchestra

The Classical orchestra had more instruments than the Baroque orchestra, so it was no longer necessary to use the harpsichord to fill out the chords. Instruments such as clarinets and French horns were added to increase the power and range of colour.

Development of the piano

The development and growing popularity of the piano meant a rise in amateur music-making in middle-class homes. Unlike the harpsichord (its Baroque ancestor), the piano could perform dynamic contrasts (loud and quiet playing) and was a much more expressive instrument. Some of the most famous pieces for piano such as *Für Elise* and the 'Moonlight' Sonata by Beethoven were written in this period.

Development of sonata form

In the Classical period the most important structure that developed was sonata form, which has three main sections:

Exposition	Here there are two main subjects or themes. The first subject is in the tonic key (chord I) and the second is often in the dominant (chord V).
Development	Here the composer plays around with the themes and explores other keys.
Recapitulation	Here the themes are restated but both in the tonic (or 'home') key.

This way of organising music was used in symphonies, concertos and sonatas, and it dominated composing in this period.

Dynamics

Dynamics were more important in the Classical period than they had been earlier. In particular, advances in instruments (such as the development of the piano) led composers to use gradual changes in volume, rather than just making sudden switches between loud and quiet.

Texture

The texture of Classical music was often more graceful and less complex than that of earlier styles. Music was often in a **homophonic** texture – where one part has the melody and the other parts accompany it. (In the previous Baroque period, textures were often more polyphonic with independent musical lines being played simultaneously.)

FACTSHEET

CLASSICAL MUSIC

THREE FAMOUS CLASSICAL COMPOSERS

Haydn (1732-1809)

Based in Vienna at the court of the Austrian emperor, Haydn wrote a wide variety of music, producing operas, symphonies, songs and string quartets. He travelled in Europe and gave concerts in London. Two of his most famous pieces are *The Creation*, an oratorio (a religious piece for orchestra, choir and soloists) and the 'Farewell' Symphony, which has the players leave the stage gradually during the last movement.

Haydn

Mozart (1756-1791)

Born in Austria to a musical father who realised his son's genius at an early age, Mozart toured Europe as a child prodigy. In his relatively short life he produced operas, symphonies, piano music, string quartets and concertos. His music is full of grace and balance and order, but his life was chaotic and he died young leaving his family without financial security despite his fame. His most famous pieces include the operas *The Magic Flute* and *The Marriage of Figaro*. Symphony No. 40, written near the end of his life, is one of the most popular symphonies ever composed.

Mozart

Beethoven (1770-1827)

Beethoven's life spanned both the Classical music era and the later Romantic period, so his music has characteristics of both. He is famous for his deafness (he went deaf at the age of 30). This hearing loss isolated him from people and society but because he found it difficult to communicate through words he used music to express his emotions instead. He composed symphonies, piano sonatas, concertos and string quartets just like Mozart and Haydn, but his pieces were longer and more intense in the way they developed musical themes.

Beethoven had an abusive childhood and never married or had children, despite falling in love with many unsuitable women. As an adult, he was a difficult, moody and shambolic-looking figure who was often mistaken for a tramp. His notated music is full of furious crossings-out and scribblings.

Beethoven

CLASSICAL MUSIC LIVES ON!

Proof of how catchy these balanced Classical melodies are even today is the number of mobile ringtones that use the main themes from Mozart's Symphony No. 40, *Eine Kleine Nachtmusik* or *Alla Turca*. The themes of Beethoven's fifth and ninth symphonies have been downloaded to thousands of phones.

A Classical string quartet

WAS MOZART MURDERED?

Mozart died young and penniless, and even today nobody is sure what he died of. However, shortly after his death, rumours grew that he had been poisoned by a rival composer called Salieri who was jealous of him. This is almost certainly untrue, but the story forms the basis of Peter Shaffer's play *Amadeus*, which later became a very successful film.

Amadeus shows the contrast between the apparent musical perfection in his pieces and his often rude and coarse personality and behaviour. Even though the film is fictitious, you can learn a lot about the Classical period from it.

WRITTEN ACTIVITIES

CLASSICAL MUSIC

1 Classical key words

Below are descriptions of musical pieces, features or composers linked to the Classical period. Match them up the correct terms in the grey box.

a) A piece of music for orchestra in four movements
b) The first section of sonata form
c) The type of texture most common in the Classical period
d) The nationality of Mozart and Haydn
e) A type of chamber music using two violins, a viola and a cello
f) A piece for solo instrument and orchestra in three movements
g) The word for volume in music
h) The composer of *The Creation*
i) The composer of *The Magic Flute*
j) An instrument added to the orchestra in the Classical period

MOZART
HAYDN
AUSTRIAN
SYMPHONY
CLARINET
EXPOSITION
HOMOPHONIC
DYNAMICS
STRING QUARTET
CONCERTO

2 Interviewing Beethoven

Here are some descriptions of Beethoven from people who met him:

'In forte [loud] passages the poor deaf man pounded on the keys until the strings jangled and in piano [quiet] he played so softly that whole groups of notes were omitted.'

Louis Spohr 1814

'A short, stout man with a very red face, bushy eyebrows...and in those small piercing eyes an expression no painter could render. It was an expression of sublimity and melancholy combined....'

An English visitor to Vienna

'He is not a man but a demon. He plays in such a way that he will drive us all to the grave.'

Audience member at a piano competition in which Beethoven had played

Imagine you are interviewing Beethoven for a magazine. Come up with ten questions you would ask him about his life and music. How do you think he would answer?

3 Promoting a musical genius

Mozart toured Europe as a boy, entertaining thousands of people even before he was a teenager. One of his concerts was on 29 June 1764 at the Ranelagh Pleasure Gardens in London. It was held to raise money for a maternity hospital.

Mozart was advertised on posters as:

'....the celebrated and astonishing Master Mozart, a Child of Seven Years of Age...'

In fact he was eight but it was more impressive to audiences if he was described as even younger than he was.

Design a poster for this concert. Remember that the main focus is the amazing child prodigy who can play like a genius on the piano. If you have access to the internet, look up some images of Mozart and London in the 1760s to use.

PRACTICAL ACTIVITIES

CLASSICAL MUSIC

1 Balanced phrasing

Play through the examples below of famous Classical question-and-answer phrases. These two melodies, composed by Mozart, use a balanced style of phrasing where the second part of the melody 'replies' to the first. See if you can play them both and then design your own question-and-answer phrases. Choose a simple key to work in (such as C major) and make sure the 'question' and 'answer' balance each other in terms of length and shape. If the first part rises then give a descending shape to the answer.

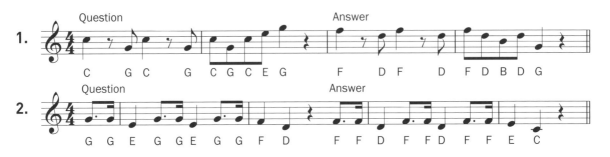

2 Alberti bass

Look below at how the chords of C major, F major and G major have had the notes broken up and placed in patterns. We call this Alberti bass. Try playing it: if you have access to a keyboard, practise it first in your right hand and then if possible in your left.

This type of pattern is typical of Classical style, grace and balance. Using this painting of a typical Classical family scene to inspire you, create a short improvisation using Alberti bass to capture the mood of the image.

Notice how carefully dressed and elegantly posed they are, and the order in the picture. The music you produce should reflect this by flowing smoothly at a steady tempo.

If you feel confident, create a melody over the top of the Alberti bass patterns. You could use your right hand for this on a piano or keyboard and keep the patterns going with your left hand underneath. If you have access to ICT, try recording the Alberti bass patterns and then adding a melody line over the top.

Classical family scene

TEACHER'S NOTES

EQUIPMENT REQUIRED

- Copies of the Factsheet to be handed out to students.
- Copies of the Written Activities worksheet to be handed out to students.
- Paper or exercise books to complete written work.
- Copies of the Practical Activities worksheet, if you feel confident in allowing students to undertake these tasks. The practical activities will require instruments (ideally keyboards or music ICT) for students to work on. Tuned percussion, guitars or the students' own instruments can also be used.
- An interactive whiteboard (optional). A PowerPoint presentation that accompanies this topic is available on the CD-ROM. This includes a reduction of the information on the factsheet and worksheets, accompanied by colour images. It also includes a link to the YouTube playlist for this topic (see below).

SUGGESTED LISTENING EXTRACTS

The following extracts are available in the YouTube playlist for this topic, which can be accessed from the PowerPoint presentation on the CD-ROM or from Rhinegold Education's YouTube channel.

- **Saint-Saëns: *Carnival of the Animals* ('The Aquarium', 'The Swan', 'The Elephant')**
- **Saint-Saëns: *Danse Macabre***
- **Wagner: 'The Ride of the Valkyries' from *Die Walküre***
- **Liszt: 'Mazeppa' Etude**
- **Paganini: Caprice No. 24**
- **Grieg: 'In the Hall of the Mountain King' from *Peer Gynt***
- **Smetana: 'Vltava' from *Má Vlast***
- **Beethoven: 'Moonlight' Sonata**

ROMANTIC MUSIC

PRIOR KNOWLEDGE

Students do not need any prior knowledge of the period and the activities can be set as an introductory or one-off lesson. You may wish to see if students have studied any music by composers such as Grieg or Schubert, such as piano pieces for grade exams studied in private music lessons. Students may also have studied Classical or 20th century music, and links can be made to these in the context of understanding general music history and development.

SUGGESTED LESSON OUTLINE

A YouTube playlist is available that contains the suggested listening extracts listed to the left. It is not essential, but it is useful to have extracts playing while the students are working.

A suggested starting activity is to play an extract and ask the class to pool their knowledge and/or views on the musical style before giving out the Factsheet. Students may well have heard or studied examples of programme music such as Saint-Saëns' *Carnival of the Animals* or *Danse Macabre*, and can be asked about music that describes something or tells a story to generate an initial discussion. Making links with humanities may also be appropriate: for example, consider links with the Industrial Revolution, revolutions in Europe, searches for national identity, and interest in the supernatural as the power of established religions started to weaken. Literary links with set texts in English literature such as Charles Dickens can help to set the scene for this topic.

You may wish students to read through the Factsheet – which contains all of the information needed to complete the tasks – individually or in pairs or small groups. The Activities worksheets can be given out with the Factsheet or afterwards.

The Activities can be undertaken in any order and some students may wish to focus on a particular one or two. If you feel confident with both the written and practical activities, you may wish to mix and match the tasks within a lesson. The material can also be split across two lessons,

TEACHER'S NOTES

ROMANTIC MUSIC

SUGGESTED LISTENING EXTRACTS (cont.)

Several of the pieces may be familiar to students ('The Ride of the Valkyries' in particular) from use in TV and films. This piece is a useful starting point for a lesson on Romantic music as it clearly shows the large orchestra, the highly charged mood and emotion, the changing dynamics and the links with myths and legends.

The Saint-Saëns piece also deals with the supernatural, with skeletons dancing a waltz (stress that this was a popular dance at the time – some students may even have experience of it through dance tuition or occasions such as weddings if they have not studied it in class).

The Liszt extract will be useful for reinforcing understanding of the term 'virtuoso', and this piece will help to set the scene musically for Written Activity 3.

You could start this lesson with a discussion of programme music (instrumental music that describes a scene or a story). Play 'The Aquarium', 'The Swan' or 'The Elephant' from Saint-Saëns' *Carnival of the Animals* and ask students which animals the music makes them think of.

SUGGESTED LESSON OUTLINE (cont.)

with the first lesson focusing on going over the Factsheet and completing the written work, and the second lesson based on the practical tasks.

Alternatively, completing two written tasks and starting off the practical work can fit within an hour-long lesson. The tasks could be completed in the next session if desired by the returning subject teacher (or the cover teacher if required).

Plenary activities can focus on key word terminology and awareness of style. Asking students to prepare three questions about the style and getting them to quiz each other is a simple follow-on activity, as is asking the class to list as many key words linked to the topic as possible without using their Factsheets.

ACTIVITY ANSWERS

Activity 1: features of Romantic music

Orchestra size	Larger than previous eras with more brass, woodwind and percussion instruments.
Dynamics	More variety in dynamics and extremes such as *ppp* and *fff*. Composers put more contrasts in their music.
Programme music	This is instrumental music that describes something or tells a story. Saint-Saëns is a good example of a composer who wrote this type of music.
The virtuoso	A genius performer who can play with amazing technical skill. Liszt was a famous virtuoso pianist.
Harmony	Chords became more complex at this time, with notes added (such as ninths) to give the harmony more colour and variety. Chromaticism and dissonance were also common.

FACTSHEET

ROMANTIC MUSIC

INTRODUCTION

Romantic music is music that was composed in the 19th century. The term 'romantic' here means expressive, or showing a range of powerful emotions and feelings, rather than just sentiments to do with love.

The 19th century was full of great changes in European society. Places such as Great Britain were becoming more industrialised and moving away from rural life; revolutions and changes in political systems were common in Europe; the growth of the middle classes resulted in a greater demand for music and other art forms to be enjoyed in the home; and more people were showing an interest in beliefs other than those of the established churches. Séances were very popular as people attempted to make contact with spirits and explore the paranormal world.

A Victorian séance

❝ ROMANTIC MUSIC SAW THE RISE OF THE VIRTUOSO, MUSICIANS WITH AMAZING TECHNIQUE WHO STUNNED AUDIENCES WITH THEIR PLAYING. ❞

19th-century industrial activity

FEATURES OF ROMANTIC MUSIC

The orchestra

The Romantic orchestra had many more players than earlier in musical history. Woodwind and brass instruments such as the cor anglais, piccolo and trombone, along with a greater variety of percussion, were added to increase the range of **timbre** and **dynamics** available to composers.

> **Timbre:** the sound quality or tone colour of the music.

> **Dynamics:** how loudly or softly the music is played.

Dynamics

The dynamic range was much greater than in earlier periods, and volume levels varied frequently within pieces. Instead of just using f (loud) or p (quiet), composers were using extremes such as fff (very very loud) or ppp (very very quiet). This could create dramatic and powerful contrasts.

Structure

Pieces were often longer and more complex in structure. A Classical period opera might take two and a half hours to perform, whereas the more extreme Romantic operas, such as those by Wagner, might be over four or five hours in length. Symphonies (orchestral pieces) also took longer to develop themes and musical ideas.

FACTSHEET

ROMANTIC MUSIC

The ascending chromatic scale: it uses all of the white and black notes in turn

Harmony

Harmony became more complex and composers were more adventurous with their chords, adding extra notes (such as ninths) to give the harmony more colour and variety. Composers also used **chromaticism** and **dissonance** in their music.

Programme music

Programme music became popular in the Romantic period, and many composers chose to write pieces in this genre. Some of them, such as Saint-Saëns' *Danse Macabre*, are still very popular today, partly because of the attraction of their storylines. (*Danse Macabre* uses music to depict the image of skeletons dancing on their graves during Halloween night.)

Nationalism

Nationalism (the love of one's country) played a major role in Romantic music. Many composers, such as Grieg, Liszt and Smetana, used folk music of their homelands in their compositions. Others such as Wagner chose to compose operas that celebrated Norse or Germanic legends – something which the Nazis in the 1930s and 1940s used to glorify their regime.

Chromaticism: moving from white to black notes in semitone steps.

Dissonance: clashing notes.

Programme music: instrumental music written to describe images, scenes, objects, stories or events.

The virtuoso

A further feature of Romantic music was the rise of the virtuoso: a musician who could demonstrate amazing technique and stun audiences with their playing. One of the most famous was the violinist Paganini. Composers wrote music especially for players such as these, and a virtuoso player in the 19th century had the status of a world-famous pop star today. They filled concert halls, went on European tours and sometimes reduced their audiences to screaming hysteria.

Brunhilde the Valkyrie – a character from Wagner's *Ring Cycle*. The *Ring Cycle* consists of four operas by Wagner based on Norse legends and has similarities in storyline to *The Lord of the Rings*.

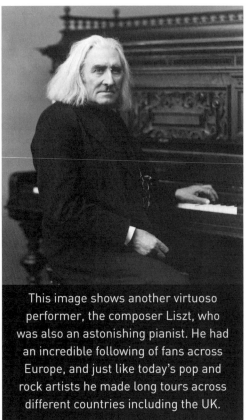

This image shows another virtuoso performer, the composer Liszt, who was also an astonishing pianist. He had an incredible following of fans across Europe, and just like today's pop and rock artists he made long tours across different countries including the UK.

WRITTEN ACTIVITIES

ROMANTIC MUSIC

1 Features of Romantic music

Under the title 'Features of the Romantic style', write a short paragraph giving information about the following:

- Orchestra size
- Dynamics
- Programme music
- The virtuoso
- Harmony

2 Romantic music wordsearch

Find the key words listed below in this Romantic music wordsearch.

a	b	u	t	o	r	c	o	g	c	s	e	e	m	h
r	r	p	n	e	t	h	d	n	h	e	t	a	t	h
e	n	t	n	t	a	o	n	f	r	r	h	r	v	a
p	p	g	s	s	i	p	e	u	o	y	a	a	i	p
o	a	r	e	e	e	i	c	f	m	b	r	e	r	l
w	s	i	i	s	h	n	s	o	a	a	p	b	t	t
n	r	d	e	b	i	c	e	c	t	r	s	h	u	o
e	r	f	a	s	h	e	r	r	i	n	e	r	o	e
t	z	s	i	l	d	r	c	o	c	m	o	a	s	v
s	a	i	n	t	s	a	e	n	s	i	a	h	o	m
o	n	a	i	p	h	p	n	t	a	m	s	n	e	o
e	c	n	a	n	o	s	s	i	d	h	t	a	y	h
z	o	i	l	r	e	b	e	a	a	e	o	v	u	d
e	r	l	l	n	d	e	n	s	f	r	s	i	g	r
a	f	e	o	l	c	o	r	a	n	g	l	a	i	s

Cor anglais	Saint-Saens	Virtuoso	Opera
Piano	Wagner	Tuba	Liszt
Chopin	Harp	Programme	Harmony
Crescendo	Dissonance	Orchestra	Dynamics

3 Promoting the virtuoso Liszt

Liszt is one of the most famous piano virtuosos. Here are some things people said about his playing:

> 'I never imagined such wonderful playing before. His hands were all over the piano; I don't believe he left a note untouched.'
>
> Alice Longfellow 1869

> 'He had finished. No one could find words. We knew not what to say or do. We could merely, as is the custom in foreign lands, kiss his hands.'
>
> Carl Lachmund 1883

Produce a poster for a concert to be given in London by Liszt on 9 June 1840 at Hanover Square Rooms in London. Use the quotations and image given here to inspire you.

A drawing of Liszt performing at a concert in Berlin to great rapture from the audience!

PRACTICAL ACTIVITIES

ROMANTIC MUSIC

1 Composing supernatural music

Romantic programme music often used the supernatural, magic and legends as a subject, as in Saint-Saëns' *Danse Macabre* and Wagner's *Ring Cycle*. To the right is a 19th-century painting based on those themes.

Create a short composition or improvisation based on this painting, using the chromatic scale (notated on the Factsheet).

You may also wish to include a diminished 7th chord:

This diminished 7th chord on C uses the notes C, E♭, F♯ and A. It is built up of minor 3rds stacked on top of each other, and is useful in creating eerie and tense music. Try combining this with the chromatic scale. Remember that silence can play a great part in building up tension and a magical atmosphere.

The Beguiling Of Merlin by Edward Burne-Jones

2 Composing watery music

Many Romantic composers depicted lakes, seas and rivers in their music by building up patterns to suggest flowing movement. One of the most famous piano pieces ever written – the 'Moonlight' Sonata by Beethoven – pictures the movement of water in music through the use of broken chords, creating a rippling effect in the right hand.

Choose a few different chords and use the notes of these to create watery effects, by building up ostinatos (repeated patterns), using broken chords (chords where the notes are played one after the other rather than together at the same time), and adding in pedal notes (long notes that are held underneath the melody). You might want to aim for something like this:

A C E C A C E C   D F A F D F A F   E C A C E C A C   D B D B D B D B

You can use different rhythms to suggest the changing speeds of the water. Decide on a programmatic theme for your music – for example, a gentle lake rippling at midnight or a river running powerfully into the sea.

TEACHER'S NOTES

JAZZ

EQUIPMENT REQUIRED

- Copies of the Factsheet to be handed out to students.
- Copies of the Written Activities worksheet to be handed out to students.
- Paper or exercise books to complete written work.
- Copies of the Practical Activities worksheet, if you feel confident in allowing students to undertake these tasks. The practical activities will require instruments (ideally keyboards or music ICT) for students to work on. Tuned percussion, guitars or the students' own instruments can also be used.
- An interactive whiteboard (optional). A PowerPoint presentation that accompanies this topic is available on the CD-ROM. This includes a reduction of the information on the factsheet and worksheets, accompanied by colour images. It also includes a link to the YouTube playlist for this topic (see below).

SUGGESTED LISTENING EXTRACTS

The following extracts are available in the YouTube playlist for this topic, which can be accessed from the PowerPoint presentation on the CD-ROM or from Rhinegold Education's YouTube channel.

- **Louis Armstrong:** *The Bare Necessities*
- **Leona Lewis:** *Summertime*
- **Scott Joplin:** *The Entertainer*
- **A trad jazz band**
- **Glen Miller:** *In The Mood*
- **Charlie Parker:** *Ko-Ko*
- **Miles Davis:** *All Blues*
- **Antonio Carlos Jobim:** *The Girl from Ipanema*
- **Ella Fitzgerald:** *One Note Samba*

PRIOR KNOWLEDGE

Most students are familiar with the basic sound of jazz, and they may well have already studied blues. In this case, draw on their understanding of the context of blues – reminding them that both jazz and blues developed in the USA within the black community. Features such as improvisation and lively offbeat rhythms are common to both styles. If students have not yet studied blues, the relevant section in this book can provide background information for the cover teacher.

SUGGESTED LESSON OUTLINE

A YouTube playlist is available that contains the suggested listening extracts listed on the left. It is not essential, but it would be useful to have extracts playing while the students are working.

A suggested starting activity is to play an extract and ask the class to pool their knowledge and/or views on the musical style before giving out the Factsheet. If this style is entirely new, playing them a classic jazz clip or even one they might know from primary school (such as Louis Armstrong's 'The Bare Necessities' from *The Jungle Book*) may be a good starting point for discussing what they already know about the style. Alternatively, you may want to start the lesson with a more recent artist covering a song in a jazz style – for example, Leona Lewis' version of *Summertime*, which featured on *The X Factor*. Some students may have studied jazz grades or played jazz pieces in their private tuition, and they may be able to talk about or even demonstrate what they know.

You may wish students to read through the Factsheet – which contains all of the information needed to complete the tasks – individually or in pairs or small groups. The Activities worksheets can be given out with the Factsheet or afterwards.

The activities can be undertaken in any order and some students may wish to focus on a particular one or two. If you feel confident

TEACHER'S NOTES

JAZZ

ACTIVITY ANSWERS

Activity 1: test your jazz knowledge

a) USA, early 1900s

b) Frontline: saxophone/trumpet/trombone/clarinet

   Rhythm section: piano/guitar/drum kit/double bass or bass guitar

c) Swing rhythm gives the music a 'bouncy' feel. Two quavers are played with the first being longer than the second. Latin music does not often use swung rhythms.

d) Ella Fitzgerald

e) Louis Armstrong or Miles Davis

f) Playing spontaneously – the music is not pre-composed

g) *The Entertainer/In the Mood/All Blues*

h) The melody or main tune

i) Trad developed before swing

SUGGESTED LESSON OUTLINE (cont.)

with both the written and practical activities, you may wish to mix and match the tasks within a lesson. The material can also be split across two lessons, with the first lesson focusing on going over the Factsheet and completing the written work, and the second lesson based on the practical tasks.

Alternatively, completing two written tasks and starting off the practical work can fit within an hour-long lesson. The tasks could be completed in the next session if desired by the returning subject teacher (or the cover teacher if required).

Plenary activities can focus on key word terminology and awareness of style. Asking students to prepare three questions about the style and getting them to quiz each other is a simple follow-on activity, as is asking the class to list as many key words linked to the topic as possible without using their Factsheets.

If practical work is not an option, breaking up the written work with audio or visual clips of performances will ensure that the class receives a solid experience of the style.

Activity 2: the features of jazz

Type of jazz	Date when this style became popular	Musical features	Famous musicians
Trad	1920s	Lively and fast with use of banjo and clarinet	Scott Joplin
Swing	1930s–1940s	Swing rhythms and bigger bands	Glenn Miller
Latin	Late 1940s	Hand-held percussion; straight rhythms; lively and fast; Brazilian and Cuban rhythms	Antonio Carlos Jobim
Cool	Late 1940s	Laid-back feel; unusual time signatures and modes	Miles Davis
Bebop	Mid-1940s	Smaller groups; dissonant harmonies; complex melodies; virtuosic solos	Charlie Parker

FACTSHEET

JAZZ

INTRODUCTION

Jazz developed in the USA in the early 1900s and is now one of America's most successful and influential musical exports. It developed from a mixture of styles, including European harmonies and African rhythms, and changed rapidly as time went on, resulting in different forms of jazz such as trad (short for traditional), swing, Latin, bebop and fusion.

> **JAZZ IS THE FOLK MUSIC OF THE MACHINE AGE.**
>
> PAUL WHITEMAN

STRAIGHT VERSUS SWING

A famous feature of many types of jazz is **swing rhythm**. This means that pairs of quavers are not played equally in length: instead, the first is a little longer than the second. This gives the rhythm a 'bouncy' feel. Not all jazz uses this – for example, Latin jazz tends to use 'straight' quavers, which means that the notes are of equal length.

> **Virtuosic:** music that is technically demanding and requires great skill to perform.

STRUCTURE OF A JAZZ PERFORMANCE

A typical jazz performance will start with a tune that all the players know. The whole band plays this tune, which is referred to as the **head**. Then some instruments will play solos, while the rhythm section accompanies with harmonies. After the solos, the band finishes with another playing of the head.

The solos will be **improvised**: made up on the spot by the players. Improvisation is one of the most important features of jazz.

A good jazz performance should feel like you have been on a journey and returned safely after exciting musical adventures.

STYLES OF JAZZ
Trad (traditional)

This is one of the earliest types of jazz and was at its most popular in the 1920s. It developed in New Orleans in Louisiana. Two common instruments used were the banjo and clarinet, and the music featured much energetic and lively playing. One of the most famous types of trad jazz is **ragtime**. Scott Joplin's ragtime piano music (his most famous tune is *The Entertainer*) is now popular all over the world due to its lively, syncopated (offbeat) rhythms and catchy melodies.

Swing

Bands became bigger in the 1930s and 1940s, and were largely made up of brass instruments (saxophones, trumpets and trombones). Swing, also known as **big band** music, was the pop music of the day. One of the best known examples of swing is *In the Mood* by Glenn Miller.

Bebop

This type of jazz developed in the mid-1940s, and was played by much smaller groups. The melodies were more complex and the harmonies more dissonant. Musicians would often play **virtuosic** solos that showed off their technical skills.

Cool

This style is what the name suggests: easy-going and laid-back. It developed in the late 1940s as a reaction against the fast, frantic feel of bebop. The music often used unusual time signatures and modes (scales that only use the white notes on a piano). Miles Davis' *All Blues* is one of the most famous pieces of cool jazz.

Latin

Latin jazz is often lively and fast. It tends to use straight rather than swung rhythms, and features hand-held percussion instruments such as the guiro, maracas and conga drums. It developed in the late 1940s and was influenced by the rhythms of Brazil and Cuba – and also Africa, because of the historical influences of slavery in those areas. The Brazilian composer, singer and guitarist Antonio Carlos Jobim is famous for his Latin music.

FACTSHEET

JAZZ

INSTRUMENTS USED IN JAZZ

Jazz bands are usually split into two sections: the frontline instruments and the rhythm section.

The **frontline** instruments play the main tune (the head) and take turns to solo. They are usually brass or woodwind instruments (saxophone, trumpet, trombone and clarinet are the most common).

The **rhythm section** accompanies the frontline instruments and provides the harmonies. It usually consists of piano and/or guitar (to play the chords), drum kit (to play the rhythm) and double bass or bass guitar (to play the bass line).

FAMOUS JAZZ MUSICIANS
Ella Fitzgerald (1917–1996)

One of the greatest jazz vocalists, Ella was famous for her scat singing. Scat is when singers use syllables such as *doo*, *wap*, and *boo* instead of words so that they can improvise without having to make up lyrics.

Ella Fitzgerald

Louis Armstrong

Louis Armstrong (1901–1971)

Born in New Orleans and nicknamed 'Satchmo', Louis became one of jazz's leading trumpeters. He is also remembered for singing the hit song 'Bare Neccessities' in Disney's *The Jungle Book*.

Charlie Parker (1920–1955)

Charlie was a saxophonist, nicknamed 'Bird', and famous for his bebop style with fast and complex improvisations. He died prematurely due to drug addiction.

Charlie Parker

Miles Davis

Miles Davis (1926–1991)

Another famous jazz trumpeter who was linked to a variety of styles – particularly cool jazz, which he pioneered. He also experimented with blending jazz with electronic music.

MUSIC COVER LESSONS

WRITTEN ACTIVITIES

JAZZ

1 Test your jazz knowledge

Answer the questions below in full sentences using the information on the Factsheet.

a) Where and when did jazz start to develop?
b) Name two frontline instruments and two rhythm section instruments.
c) Describe swing rhythm, and name a type of jazz that tends **not** to use it.
d) Name a famous jazz vocalist.
e) Name a famous jazz trumpeter.
f) What does 'improvisation' mean?
g) Name a famous jazz tune.
h) What does the term 'head' mean in jazz?
i) Which style developed first – trad jazz or swing?

2 The features of jazz

Fill in the blanks in the table below.

Type of jazz	Date when this style became popular	Musical features	Famous musicians
Trad			Scott Joplin
Swing	1930s – 1940s		
Latin		Hand-held percussion; straight rhythms; lively and fast; Brazilian and Cuban rhythms	
Cool			Miles Davis
Bebop	Mid-1940s		

3 Describing jazz

Imagine you are describing jazz to someone who has never heard it before. Decide on the main points and produce a guide to jazz on an A4 sheet. Remember to include key words, facts on famous performers, the instruments used and features of different jazz styles. If you have time, illustrate your guide with some images.

PRACTICAL ACTIVITIES

JAZZ

1 Bass line and melody composition

This task combines two musical lines (a bass line and a melody), so you will need to choose whether to work on it individually or in pairs.

Start off with a jazz bass line (such as the one shown below) played steadily over and over again. If you are using a piano or keyboard, you can play it in both hands in octaves if you wish. If you are sharing a keyboard with someone else, this should be played in the left-hand lower part. On a computer or an electric keyboard use a bass sound.

Jazz trumpeter Miles Davis

Now with either your right hand (keeping the bass line going in your left) or with the other person taking this role, use notes from the blues scale in the key of A (shown below) to play some rhythmic patterns over the bass line. Aim for syncopated (offbeat) rhythms and use repetition as jazz players do. Remember that sometimes the most effective melodies use just a few notes.

If you want a challenge, you could add in occasional chords in the bass such as A minor (A C E), G major (G B D) and F major (F A C).

2 Experimenting with scat singing

If possible, listen to an example of scat singing by Ella Fitzgerald. *One Note Samba* is a good example. Notice the sorts of syllables she uses to improvise with, for example:

Doo   Shoo   Ba   Wap   Boo

Now experiment with improvising a vocal line using syllables like these. You could play the bass line given below as an accompaniment to your scat singing.

Either play the bass line yourself and sing over the top, or ask someone else to play the bass line while you sing. The bass-line player could also add in the chords (written above the music) if they wish.

Time yourself scat singing: can you keep going for 30 seconds? How about even longer?

TEACHER'S NOTES

BLUES

EQUIPMENT REQUIRED

- Copies of the Factsheet to be handed out to students.
- Copies of the Written Activities worksheet to be handed out to students.
- Paper or exercise books to complete written work.
- Copies of the Practical Activities worksheet, if you feel confident in allowing students to undertake these tasks. The practical activities will require instruments (ideally keyboards or music ICT) for students to work on. Tuned percussion, guitars or the students' own instruments can also be used.
- An interactive whiteboard (optional). A PowerPoint presentation that accompanies this topic is available on the CD-ROM. This includes a reduction of the information on the factsheet and worksheets, accompanied by colour images. It also includes a link to the YouTube playlist for this topic (see below).

SUGGESTED LISTENING EXTRACTS

The following extracts are available in the YouTube playlist for this topic, which can be accessed from the PowerPoint presentation on the CD-ROM or from Rhinegold Education's YouTube channel.

- Amy Winehouse: *Wake Up Alone*
- Katie Melua: *Blues in the Night*
- Bessie Smith: *St. Louis Blues*
- Blind Lemon Jefferson: *Hangman's Blues*
- Wynton Marsalis: *Happy Birthday improvisation*
- Gershwin: *Rhapsody in Blue*
- Miles Davis: 'All Blues' from *Kind of Blue*
- Elvis Presley: *Jailhouse Rock*
- Moby: 'Natural Blues' from *Play*

PRIOR KNOWLEDGE

The activities for this topic do not require any previous study of blues music, and can be set as a first lesson. You may wish to see if students have already studied jazz: there are a number of links that can be made between the two styles, such as their development in the early 20th century among the black community in the USA.

SUGGESTED LESSON OUTLINE

A YouTube playlist is available that contains the suggested listening extracts listed on the left. It is not essential, but it would be useful to have extracts playing while the students are working.

A suggested starting activity is to link this music to a more contemporary blues-influenced artist, such as Amy Winehouse. When Amy died in 2011, Lady Gaga said of her:

> 'Amy changed pop music forever. I remember knowing there was hope, and feeling not alone because of her. She lived jazz; she lived the blues.'

Students can be encouraged to discuss Amy Winehouse's singing and its emotional style, which harks back to the early blues singers of the 1920s.

You may wish students to read through the Factsheet – which contains all of the information needed to complete the tasks – individually or in pairs or small groups. The Activities worksheets can be given out with the Factsheet or afterwards.

The activities can be undertaken in any order and some students may wish to focus on a particular one or two. If you feel confident with both the written and practical activities, you may wish to mix and match the tasks within a lesson. The material can also be split across two lessons, with the first lesson focusing on going over the Factsheet and completing the written work, and the second lesson based on the practical tasks.

TEACHER'S NOTES

ACTIVITY ANSWERS

Activity 1: fill in the blanks

Here is the text that students are asked to complete in Written Activity 1, with the missing words added in bold.

Blues developed in the Afro-American community in the **USA** in the 1900s. It was primarily a vocal genre that was accompanied in a simple style by instruments such as the banjo or **harmonica**.

Blues has a **12**-bar chord **pattern** and the scale uses flattened or **blue** notes, which give it a distinctive sound. Another feature of blues is the offbeat rhythms or **syncopation**, which clearly show an African influence.

The verses in blues songs were often in **AAB** form with the first line being repeated.

A white American composer who led the way for many others by using a blues influence in his music was **Gershwin**. One of his most famous pieces, ***Rhapsody in Blue***, shows how this style can be fused with Western classical music.

BLUES

SUGGESTED LESSON OUTLINE (cont.)

Alternatively, completing two written tasks and starting off the practical work can fit within an hour-long lesson. The tasks could be completed in the next session if desired by the returning subject teacher (or the cover teacher if required).

Plenary activities can focus on key word terminology and awareness of style. Asking students to prepare three questions about the style and getting them to quiz each other is a good concluding activity, as is asking the class to list as many key words linked to the topic as possible without using their Factsheets.

If practical work is not an option, breaking up the written work with audio or visual clips of performances will ensure that the class receives a solid experience of the style.

FACTSHEET

BLUES

INTRODUCTION

Blues is one of the most important musical styles of the 20th century. The genre began as a form of black American folk music, and it has influenced popular music ever since it developed. Blues artists range from Bessie Smith (1894–1937) to Amy Winehouse (1983–2011). These two singers have more in common than you might think – both were considered to be great blues performers.

> ❝ AMY WINEHOUSE CHANGED POP MUSIC FOREVER. I REMEMBER KNOWING THERE WAS HOPE, AND FEELING NOT ALONE BECAUSE OF HER. SHE LIVED JAZZ; SHE LIVED THE BLUES. ❞
>
> **LADY GAGA**

Amy Winehouse

Bessie Smith

FEATURES OF THE BLUES

- Most blues pieces are based on a **12-bar chord pattern** that – in its simplest form – just uses three main chords. Here is the chord pattern in C major:

1	2	3	4	5	6	7	8	9	10	11	12
C⁷	C⁷	C⁷	C⁷	F⁷	F⁷	C⁷	C⁷	G⁷	F⁷	C⁷	C⁷

(Note that all of these chords have the seventh note added to them: B♭ for C major, E♭ for F major and F♮ for G major.)

- Most blues pieces have a **time signature** of $\frac{4}{4}$, but there are also some famous examples of blues waltzes in $\frac{3}{4}$.

- Blues music uses the blues scale, which has flattened notes that are also called **blue notes**:

- Blues music is often **syncopated** (it uses offbeat rhythms). This aspect of the music is a result of its **African** origins: the earliest blues singers were descended from the African slaves who were brought to the USA to work. A good example of a famous 'straight' tune being played in a syncopated manner is Wynton Marsalis' version of *Happy Birthday*, which you can find on YouTube. It is clearly the same tune but the rhythms have been made offbeat (syncopated).

- Early blues often had a **strophic** structure, which simply means that one verse is followed by another and another. Each verse often had an **AAB** shape: the first two lines would be the same and the third line would usually rhyme with the first. For example:

  Hangman's rope sho' is tough and strong (A)
  Hangman's rope sho' is tough and strong (A)
  They gonna hang me because I done something wrong (B)
  (Blind Lemon Jefferson)

EARLY BLUES INSTRUMENTS

Early blues was principally a vocal genre that didn't rely on sophisticated instrumental accompaniments. The main instruments were ones that were available cheaply (such as the **banjo** or **harmonica**), or instruments that could provide a strong chordal accompaniment (such as the **guitar** or **piano**).

FACTSHEET

BLUES

BLUES MEETS CLASSICAL

One of the most important figures in helping to establish the blues as a musical style to be taken seriously was the white American composer **George Gershwin**. A highly trained classical composer, his music is full of the influences of blues and jazz: syncopated rhythms, blue notes and the blues chord pattern. Two of his most famous compositions are the opera *Porgy and Bess* and the orchestral piece *Rhapsody in Blue* which, as the title suggests, has the blues style running all the way through it right from the opening clarinet melody to the final crashing chords.

BLUES MEETS JAZZ

Miles Davis' *Kind of Blue* (1959)

Blues and jazz both developed in the black community in the early 20th century. They share many features such as syncopated rhythms, similar instrumentation and use of improvisation. The early blues and jazz artists learned their music and skills through listening and copying rather than from reading notation. Some jazz artists took up the blues scale and chord pattern: for example, the famous jazz trumpeter Miles Davis made an album called *Kind of Blue*, which features a small jazz band that plays blues melodies in a jazz style, and improvises solos over the blues chord pattern.

BLUES MEETS ROCK'N'ROLL

Elvis Presley's *Jailhouse Rock* (1957)

This classic rock'n'roll song is a great example of how the blues style influenced later forms of popular music. White artists such as Elvis Presley started to contribute to what was originally just a black style of music. This song, with its blues chord pattern and singing style, had a huge influence on vocalists of the 1950s and 1960s.

BLUES MEETS DANCE MUSIC

'Natural Blues' from Moby's *Play* (2000)

Many dance artists have used the blues style in their tracks, and some have sampled authentic blues recordings. An interesting example of this is 'Natural Blues' from the album *Play*. Moby took a sample from a 1950s recording of an American blues singer performing *Trouble So Hard*, and used this melody line over a modern dance beat and bass line.

What are blues songs about?

Early blues songs often acted as a type of social commentary about how hard people's lives could be. Figures such as Howlin' Wolf and Bessie Smith sang about the racial discrimination and hardship that all Afro-Americans faced in the early 20th century. Other themes included love songs (usually love gone wrong), unemployment, natural disasters and injustice.

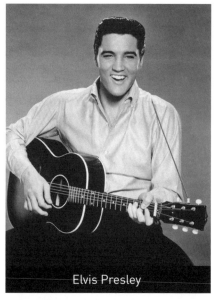

Elvis Presley

Moby

WRITTEN ACTIVITIES

BLUES

1 Fill in the blanks

Write out and complete the text below, which contains basic facts about the blues style. Fill in the blanks with the words given below.

Blues developed in the Afro-American community in the _____ in the 1900s. It was primarily a vocal genre that was accompanied in a simple style by instruments such as the banjo or _____.

Blues has a _____-bar chord _____ and the scale uses flattened or _____ notes, which give it a distinctive sound. Another feature of blues is the offbeat rhythm or _____ which clearly shows an African influence.

The verses in blues songs were often in _____ form with the first line being repeated.

A white American composer who led the way for many others by using a blues influence in his music was _____. One of his most famous pieces, _____, shows how this style can be fused with Western classical music.

GERSHWIN   SYNCOPATION   RHAPSODY IN BLUE   USA
HARMONICA   BLUE   AAB   PATTERN   12

2 Write a music quiz

Write a music quiz based on the following key words about the blues. Each question should have one of the following key words or phrases as an answer. Once you have written your questions, quiz a friend to see if they can guess the right answers. An example has been completed for you.

Improvisation   Strophic
Banjo   12-bar chord pattern
Amy Winehouse   *Jailhouse Rock*
Harmonica   George Gershwin
Syncopation

Example:
Question: what word describes the offbeat rhythms commonly used in blues music?
Answer: syncopation.

3 Writing blues lyrics

Using the song form AAB, write some verses to a blues song about an event that has made an impact on you. This could be:

- A natural disaster such as a storm or flood
- The death of a celebrity or person of influence
- Something important that happened in your life.

Remember to use the AAB shape and aim to make the third line rhyme with the other two. Look back at the passage on strophic form on the Factsheet for help.

PRACTICAL ACTIVITIES　　　　　　　　　　BLUES

1 Playing a blues chord sequence

Play through the blues chord pattern in C major. You may wish to play three-note chords using just the white notes, or you could add the seventh notes in too (these are the blue notes). Make sure the chords last for four beats each, and experiment with playing them in different rhythmic patterns.

1	2	3	4	5	6	7	8	9	10	11	12
C⁷	C⁷	C⁷	C⁷	F⁷	F⁷	C⁷	C⁷	G⁷	F⁷	C⁷	C⁷

C⁷ = C E G B♭　　　　**F⁷** = F A C E♭　　　　**G⁷** = G B D F

Guitarists may prefer to use the key of A. Here is a 12-bar blues chord pattern in A:

1	2	3	4	5	6	7	8	9	10	11	12
A⁷	A⁷	A⁷	A⁷	D⁷	D⁷	A⁷	A⁷	E⁷	D⁷	A⁷	A⁷

2 Composing a blues melody

Play through the blues scale starting on C. Check you are using the correct black notes:

C　E♭　F　G♭　G♮　B♭　C

Now you have played it through, start improvising with it. Build up short patterns and repeat them – remember that blues music uses syncopated rhythms. Then work on developing a blues melody in an AAB shape as follows:

A: Compose a first phrase that lasts for 2 bars (8 beats).

A: Once you are happy with it, repeat it once.

B: Now compose a second phrase that also lasts for 2 bars, but contrasts with the first one.

If you have already completed the first activity above, you may want to compose this melody so it fits with the blues chord pattern. This means that the notes you use need to match the chords in the pattern. You could then perform your melody over the chord pattern, using this structure:

1	2	3	4	5	6	7	8	9	10	11	12
C⁷	C⁷	C⁷	C⁷	F⁷	F⁷	C⁷	C⁷	G⁷	F⁷	C⁷	C⁷
Phrase A		Rest		Phrase A		Rest		Phrase B		Rest	

TEACHER'S NOTES

EQUIPMENT REQUIRED

- Copies of the Factsheet to be handed out to students.
- Copies of the Written Activities worksheet to be handed out to students.
- Paper or exercise books to complete written work.
- Copies of the Practical Activities worksheet, if you feel confident in allowing students to undertake these tasks. The practical activities will require instruments (ideally keyboards or music ICT) for students to work on. Tuned percussion, guitars or the students' own instruments can also be used.
- An interactive whiteboard (optional). A PowerPoint presentation that accompanies this topic is available on the CD-ROM. This includes a reduction of the information on the factsheet and worksheets, accompanied by colour images. It also includes a link to the YouTube playlist for this topic (see below).

SUGGESTED LISTENING EXTRACTS

The following extracts are available in the YouTube playlist for this topic, which can be accessed from the PowerPoint presentation on the CD-ROM or from Rhinegold Education's YouTube channel.

- Laura Marling: *Rambling Man*
- Mumford & Sons: *Little Lion Man*
- Bellowhead: *Prickle Eye Bush*
- Martin Carthy: *Scarborough Fair*
- The Imagined Village: *Scarborough Fair*
- Chris Wood and Andy Cutting
- Vaughan Williams: *The Lark Ascending*
- Thin Lizzy: *Whiskey in the Jar*
- Billy Bragg: *Which Side Are You On*
- Chris Wood: *The Grand Correction*

BRITISH FOLK MUSIC

PRIOR KNOWLEDGE

The activities for this topic do not rely on students having any prior knowledge of folk music. However, you may want to remind students of modes, the scales commonly used in folk music, if they have previously covered medieval music or jazz. Many students may already know the notes to the Aeolian and Dorian modes (see below).

If modes are new to the class, you could explain that they are types of scales that were used in Western music before the development of major and minor keys. They are still used today in styles such as folk music and world music.

The Aeolian mode uses all of the white notes on the piano from A to A:

The Dorian mode uses all of the white notes from D to D:

SUGGESTED LESSON OUTLINE

Folk music has undergone a renaissance in the last few decades in the UK. Artists such as Mumford & Sons, Bellowhead and Laura Marling may be familiar to students. Some students may be personally involved or have family links with the folk scene and you may be able to draw on these.

If internet access allows, a useful starting point may be to play an extract from the YouTube playlist of a contemporary folk artist (such as Laura Marling or Mumford & Sons) and ask the class for comments on the music. Can they identify what style it is?

Follow this with a more traditional folk performance. *Scarborough Fair* by Martin Carthy is a good starting point as it is such a famous folk song and many students will recognise it. (You could contrast this with the version by The Imagined Village, which is a more contemporary interpretation that includes a sitar.) The extract

TEACHER'S NOTES

ACTIVITY ANSWERS

Activity 1: fill in the blanks

Here is the text that the students are asked to complete in Written Activity 1, with the missing words added in bold.

Folk music is nearly always learnt through the **oral tradition**. Instead of major and minor keys it often uses old-fashioned scales called **modes**. Folk songs often have a structure of verse followed by verse, the same tune being repeated: we call this **strophic** form. Songs are often sung solo without accompaniment (which is called a **monophonic** texture).

Instruments commonly used in British folk music include the **melodeon**, **fiddle** and the **bagpipes**. The harp is particularly linked to the folk music of **Wales**. As well as songs, there is a rich tradition of instrumental dances such as the **jig** and the **reel**. A leading figure who wrote down many of these tunes was **Cecil Sharp**.

BRITISH FOLK MUSIC

SUGGESTED LESSON OUTLINE (cont.)

in the playlist of Chris Wood and Andy Cutting is also a good introduction to traditional folk music.

You could ask students about how this music is taught and passed on from generation to generation. Some may already know (from a study of world music) the term 'oral tradition'.

You may wish students to read through the Factsheet – which contains all of the information needed to complete the tasks – individually or in pairs or small groups. The Activities worksheets can be given out with the Factsheet or afterwards.

The activities can be undertaken in any order and some students may wish to focus on a particular one or two. If you feel confident with both the written and practical activities, you may wish to mix and match the tasks within a lesson. The material can also be split across two lessons, with the first lesson focusing on going over the Factsheet and completing the written work, and the second lesson based on the practical tasks.

Alternatively, completing two written tasks and starting off the practical work can fit within an hour-long lesson. The tasks could be completed in the next session if desired by the returning subject teacher (or the cover teacher if required).

Plenary activities can focus on key word terminology and awareness of style. Asking students to prepare three questions about the style and getting them to quiz each other is a good concluding activity, as is asking the class to list as many key words linked to the topic as possible without using their Factsheets.

If practical work is not an option, breaking up the written work with audio or visual clips of performances will ensure that the class receives a solid experience of the style.

FACTSHEET

BRITISH FOLK MUSIC

INTRODUCTION

British folk music refers to traditional music from Britain that, in the past, was performed by the 'folk' – the lower rather than upper classes. Until the 20th century and the start of recorded sound, it was the type of music that most people heard, played and sang. It was not usually written down. The traditional lifestyles that featured in many folk songs started to disappear as Britain became more industrialised during the 19th century, and folk music was in danger of dying out altogether. However, there is now a very healthy and active folk music scene and a whole new generation of artists is keeping the British folk tradition alive.

> ❝ A WHOLE NEW GENERATION OF ARTISTS IS KEEPING THE BRITISH FOLK TRADITION ALIVE. ❞

Mumford & Sons

Bellowhead

TWO GREAT FIGURES IN BRITISH FOLK MUSIC

Ralph Vaughan Williams (1872–1958)

One of the greatest English composers, Vaughan Williams collected folk tunes and used them in his music, sometimes re-arranging them and sometimes using them to inspire his own music. Two of his best known pieces are *Fantasia on Greensleeves*, in which he arranged the famous folk song for orchestra, and *The Lark Ascending*, where the music describes a bird soaring in the air on a beautiful summer's day.

Vaughan Williams

Cecil Sharp (1859–1924)

A composer and teacher, Cecil Sharp is chiefly remembered for travelling around Britain, Europe and the USA collecting folk tunes. He recorded these tunes or wrote them down so they could still be remembered in years to come.

KEY WORDS

Strophic	Songs that use verses one after the other which are set to the same melody. This is a very common structure in folk music.
Mode	Scales that were used before the development of major and minor scales. You may have studied the Aeolian and Dorian modes in jazz or medieval music.
Drone	Repeated or sustained notes, often at intervals of a 5th, played as an accompaniment. The bagpipes are a type of folk instrument that have a built-in drone.
Oral tradition	Music learnt through listening and copying. In the past many people who sang and played folk music could not read or write notation.

INSTRUMENTS USED IN BRITISH FOLK

Different instruments are popular in different parts of Britain for playing folk music (although there is a lot of overlap between them). For example, the **tin whistle** and **bagpipes** are common in Scottish folk music, the **harp** in Welsh folk music and the **melodeon** and **guitar** in English folk music. The **fiddle** (or violin) is a popular folk instrument throughout Britain.

FACTSHEET

BRITISH FOLK MUSIC

TYPES OF BRITISH FOLK MUSIC

Ballads	Songs that tell a story.
Shanties	Songs connected to the sea, sailors and ships. One of the most famous is *What Shall We Do With The Drunken Sailor*.
Jigs	Lively dances with a time signature of $\frac{6}{8}$.
Reels	Dances with a fast tempo and a $\frac{4}{4}$ time signature.
Morris dances	Lively melodies used for morris dancing (a type of English folk dance).
Ceilidh bands	Folk bands that play Scottish tunes for ceilidhs (a type of social gathering where everyone can join in with the dances).
Welsh harp airs (Penillion airs)	Welsh folk tunes sung over a harp accompaniment.
Unaccompanied folk singing	Many folk songs in the past were sung unaccompanied.

TEXTURE IN BRITISH FOLK MUSIC

Much folk music in the past was sung by a solo voice (or in unison) without any accompaniment or harmony. This type of texture is **monophonic**. Sometimes harmonies would be added, especially in the choruses. This is called a **homophonic** texture. Another type of texture is **heterophonic**. This means that while the main tune is being played or sung, other people will join in with it but decorate and embellish it (for example by adding in ornaments). The result is that slightly different versions of the tune are heard at the same time.

Melodeon

WHAT ARE FOLK SONGS ABOUT?

One of the most important aspects of a folk song is that it tells a story. Many folk songs act as a type of commentary on different aspects of life or topical events. Originally, folk songs were often about people's work and lives in small farming communities, and later about life during the industrial revolution. Some songs tell us of broken love affairs or sailors going off to sea and coming back years later to find their wife or girlfriend has found another man. True-life gritty subjects such as murders, executions, unwanted pregnancies and robberies by highwaymen all feature in folk songs.

FOLK FUSION

It is now common to find British folk songs performed in different styles – for example jazz, classical, rock and pop. When musical styles are joined together like this we call it a **fusion**. One example of a famous folk fusion song is Thin Lizzy's 1973 hit *Whiskey in the Jar* – a rock version of a folk song that is hundreds of years old.

Monophonic: the simplest type of texture where there is just one melody line and no accompaniment.

Homophonic: where one part has the melody and the other parts provide chords or harmony.

Heterophonic: where different versions of the same melody are heard simultaneously.

WRITTEN ACTIVITIES

BRITISH FOLK MUSIC

1 Fill in the blanks

Read through the Factsheet and then complete the text below about British folk music.

Folk music is nearly always learnt through the _____ _____. Instead of major and minor keys it often uses old-fashioned scales called _____. Folk songs often have a structure of verse followed by verse, the same tune being repeated: we call this _____ form. Songs are often sung solo without accompaniment (which is called a _____ texture).

Instruments commonly used in British folk music include the _____, _____ and the _____. The harp is particularly linked to the folk music of _____. As well as songs, there is a rich tradition of instrumental dances such as the _____ and the _____. A leading figure who wrote down many of these tunes was _____ _____.

CECIL SHARP   MELODEON   STROPHIC   ORAL TRADITION
JIG   WALES   REEL   MONOPHONIC   FIDDLE   BAGPIPES   MODES

2 Writing down folk music

Imagine you are a farmworker in 1902 in rural England. The composer Ralph Vaughan Williams turns up at your local pub, buys drinks and persuades you and your fellow villagers to sing songs which he writes down.

Write a diary entry or a letter to a friend which describes this event. If you want to extend this idea, turn this piece of writing into a short story about a farm worker who meets the composer! Describe what happens, how you feel about singing to this gentleman, and how the other villagers react. What would the songs be about? Would you feel this was a useful thing for the composer to be doing?

3 Key words about folk music

Make a list of 20 key words linked to the topic of British folk music. Use these words to create either a spider diagram or a word search. If you have time, illustrate some of these key words either on the spider diagram itself or on the other side of the word search.

PRACTICAL ACTIVITIES

BRITISH FOLK MUSIC

1 Composing a melody with the Aeolian mode

Using the Aeolian mode (the white notes on a piano from A to A – see below), make up a melody suitable for dancing to at a harvest supper. As you are writing a dance tune, your melody should be lively, use repetition and have a strong sense of beat. You may wish to structure it with an AABA shape (i.e. write one phrase, repeat it, write a contrasting phrase and then repeat the first one again).

If you want to add an accompaniment, you could use the following chords (which only use the white notes on a keyboard):

Am	**G**	**F**	**Dm**	**C**
(A C E)	(G B D)	(F A C)	(D F A)	(C E G)

Make sure the start of the piece uses the note A or the chord Am to establish the mode.

2 Writing a folk song

Folk music was originally a way in which ordinary people could sing about their lives, their work and the issues that affected them. This tradition has carried on for hundreds of years. In the 1960s, singers in the USA such as Joan Baez and Bob Dylan reached audiences worldwide with protest songs about issues such as civil rights and the Vietnam war. In the UK, songwriter Billy Bragg started writing music in the 1980s about Thatcherism, the miners' strike and the Falklands War. He is still writing songs about similar issues today.

What makes you angry about society? Which political or social issue do you feel strongly about?

What is one of the most important things that people of your age face? Is it one of the following?

BULLYING   UNEMPLOYMENT
GLOBAL WARMING   KNIFE CRIME

All of these topics would make a suitable subject for a contemporary folk song. On your own or in pairs, choose a topic and develop some lyrics. Can you structure it in a strophic form (verse followed by verse?) If you have time, you could then write a melody to fit your lyrics that uses the notes of the Aeolian or Dorian mode.

If you can, listen to *The Grand Correction* by Chris Wood as an example of a folk song which deals with a contemporary issue (this song is about the 2008 financial crisis).

TEACHER'S NOTES

REGGAE

EQUIPMENT REQUIRED

- Copies of the Factsheet to be handed out to students.
- Copies of the Written Activities worksheet to be handed out to students.
- Paper or exercise books to complete written work.
- Copies of the Practical Activities worksheet, if you feel confident in allowing students to undertake these tasks. The practical activities will require instruments (ideally keyboards or music ICT) for students to work on. Tuned percussion, guitars or the students' own instruments can also be used.
- An interactive whiteboard (optional). A PowerPoint presentation that accompanies this topic is available on the CD-ROM. This includes a reduction of the information on the factsheet and worksheets, accompanied by colour images. It also includes a link to the YouTube playlist for this topic (see below).

SUGGESTED LISTENING EXTRACTS

The following extracts are available in the YouTube playlist for this topic, which can be accessed from the PowerPoint presentation on the CD-ROM or from Rhinegold Education's YouTube channel.

- Bob Marley: *One Love*
- Bob Marley: *Buffalo Soldier*
- Bob Marley: *Exodus*
- Haile Selassie in London
- Haile Selassie in Jamaica
- Bobby McFerrin: *Don't Worry Be Happy*
- The Police: *Walking on the Moon*
- Blondie: *The Tide is High*
- Stevie Wonder: *Happy Birthday*
- Rihanna: *Man Down*
- Dizzee Rascal: *Can't Tek No More*

The most obvious tracks to play to illustrate the style (and the most immediately recognisable) are Bob Marley's songs: *One Love*, *Buffalo Soldier* and *Exodus*. These three also illustrate some of the main themes of his music: peace, equality and struggle. The clip of Haile Selassie in London can help students to put in

PRIOR KNOWLEDGE

The activities for this topic do not require any previous study of reggae. They can be set as an introductory or one-off lesson. Many students will instantly recognise the reggae style, and links can also be made to blues or jazz if the class has already studied these topics.

Reggae is a style of popular music that developed among the black community in Jamaica during the 1960s. Students should be encouraged to discuss any personal links with Jamaica and/or their experience of the country.

Some students may also have covered Rastafari in Religious Studies, which is an important aspect of reggae music, and may also be familiar with Bob Marley's life and music.

SUGGESTED LESSON OUTLINE

A YouTube playlist is available that contains the suggested listening extracts listed to the left. It is not essential, but it is useful to have extracts playing while the students are working.

A suggested starting activity is to play an extract and ask the class to pool their knowledge and/or views on the musical style before giving out the Factsheet. If the cover work is being set as a revision exercise on a previously studied topic, this will be particularly valuable.

You may wish students to read through the Factsheet – which contains all of the information needed to complete the tasks – individually or in pairs or small groups. The Activities worksheets can be given out with the Factsheet or afterwards.

The activities can be undertaken in any order and some students may wish to focus on a particular one or two. If you feel confident with both the written and practical activities, you may wish to mix and match the tasks within a lesson.

TEACHER'S NOTES

REGGAE

SUGGESTED LISTENING EXTRACTS (cont.)

context the information on Rastafari, and clarifies the emperor's position and importance. The clip of Selassie arriving in Jamaica can help you to stress how Rastafari was a rapidly growing religion, later made world-famous by Bob Marley and his music.

The Bobby McFerrin track is a great example of not just reggae but a cappella singing and vocal percussion as well. If you feel confident in getting groups to work with body percussion and vocals, students could try to imitate this performance.

The last five tracks in the playlist – ranging from The Police to Dizzee Rascal – show the influence of reggae from the 1970s to now.

ACTIVITY ANSWERS

Activity 1: fill in the blanks

Reggae is music from **Jamaica** that developed in the **1960s**. Reggae's musical influences include types of Caribbean music such as **ska** and **mento**. Reggae always has **four** steady beats in each bar but the rhythms are often offbeat. The word for this is **syncopation**. The most famous reggae artist is **Bob Marley** who followed the religion **Rastafari**.

Activity 2: Reggae instruments

Instrument	Role in reggae music
Drum kit	Rhythm
Bass guitar	Bass line or riffs
Saxophone	Riffs or chords
Trumpet	Riffs or chords
Organ	Chords

SUGGESTED LESSON OUTLINE (cont.)

The material can also be split across two lessons, with the first lesson focusing on going over the Factsheet and completing the written work, and the second lesson based on the practical tasks.

Alternatively, completing two written tasks and starting off the practical work can fit within an hour-long lesson. The tasks could be completed in the next session if desired by the returning subject teacher (or the cover teacher if required).

Plenary activities can focus on key word terminology and awareness of style. Asking students to prepare three questions about the style and getting them to quiz each other is a simple follow-up activity, as is asking the class to list as many key words linked to the topic as possible without using the Factsheets.

If practical work is not an option, breaking up the written work with audio or visual clips of performances will ensure that the class receives a solid experience of the style.

FACTSHEET

REGGAE

INTRODUCTION

Reggae music is one of Jamaica's greatest exports. It developed there in the 1960s, and ever since Bob Marley brought it to a worldwide audience, it has remained a much-loved style enjoyed by people of all ages.

MUSICAL FEATURES

Reggae developed from a mixture of musical genres. These included Jamaican popular styles such as ska, mento and rocksteady; rhythm and blues from the USA; and traditional African rhythms, which all fused together to create the immediately recognisable features of reggae. These include:

- The **syncopated** offbeat rhythm, in which the second and fourth beats in the bar are emphasised:

- A $\frac{4}{4}$ time signature.
- Simple and repetitive chord patterns and melodies.
- Prominent bass guitar **riffs**.
- A laid-back tempo and feel.

Reggae lyrics are often about political issues such as equal rights. Bob Marley's songs also celebrated his religion, Rastafari.

Riff: a repeated melodic or rhythmic pattern. First used in jazz, riffs are now common in pop, rock and world music.

RASTAFARI

To understand reggae fully you need to know about the religion of Rastafari and what Rastafarians believe.

Rastafarians believe that a past emperor of Ethiopia, **Haile Selassie**, was God, and that Ethiopia is the spiritual and true home for all black people. They refer to Ethiopia as **Zion**: a place that will bring unity, peace and freedom to Rastafarians. The opposite of Zion is **Babylon**, which essentially refers to white Western society. Rastafarians choose to wear dreadlocks as they believe the Bible commands them to never cut their hair, and they wear knitted caps in the Ethiopian colours: red, gold and green. A controversial aspect of Rastafari is the belief that smoking cannabis will bring you closer to God (Jah).

The religion developed initially as an exclusively black movement, with a focus on issues within the black community such as equal rights, but there are now Rastafarians all over the world and from different ethnic backgrounds.

Bob Marley

Even decades after his death in 1981, Bob Marley is still the world's most famous Rastafarian. He converted after meeting his first wife, Rita. The religion had an enormous influence on his life and his music. The lyrics below from Bob Marley's song *Exodus* refer to some of the features of Rastafari:

> 'We the generation
> trod through great tribulation
> Exodus: movement of Jah people
> Open your eyes and look within
> Are you satisfied with the life you're living?
> We know where we're going; we know where we're from
> We're leaving Babylon, we're going to our fatherland . . .'

His most famous songs include *Exodus*, *One Love*, *I Shot the Sheriff*, *Trenchtown Rock*, *Buffalo Soldier* and *Three Little Birds*.

Bob Marley's legacy lives on in many ways. There is a Bob Marley Museum and Foundation in Jamaica, and several of his 11 children, including Ziggy and Damian, are successful performers in their own right. Most importantly, his songs are downloaded and played across the world every day.

FACTSHEET

REGGAE

BOB MARLEY LIFELINE

1945	Born 'Nesta Robert Marley' to a black mother and a white father. He was brought up on a rural farm in Jamaica but moved to Kingston when he was a teenager.
1963	Bob's first band, The Wailing Wailers, is formed.
mid-1960s	Bob converts from Christianity to Rastafari.
1971	Bob gets a contract with Island Records, after an unsuccessful tour leaves him stranded and broke in London.
1974	Eric Clapton records a cover of *I Shot The Sheriff* that becomes an American hit, helping to raise Bob's international profile.
1976	Bob's political leanings result in an assassination attempt on his life.
1977	Bob works on the album *Exodus* while living in London in self-imposed exile.
1981	Bob dies of cancer in Florida.

Where does the word reggae come from?

The word 'reggae' was first coined when a Jamaican band called The Maytals released a single in 1968 called *Do the Reggay*. The lead singer of The Maytals said this about reggae music:

> 'Reggae just mean comin' from the people, an everyday thing, like from the ghetto. When you say reggae you mean *regular*, majority. And when you say reggae it means poverty, suffering, Rastafari, everything in the ghetto.'

Bob Marley's son Ziggy performing

REGGAE INFLUENCE

All of these songs display reggae influences, despite being written in different decades and performed by different artists:

- *Walking on the Moon* by The Police
- *The Tide is High* by Blondie
- *Happy Birthday* by Stevie Wonder
- *Don't Worry Be Happy* by Bobby McFerrin
- *Man Down* by Rihanna
- *Can't Tek No More* by Dizzee Rascal

INSTRUMENTS USED IN REGGAE

As well as the basic rock or pop line up of drum kit, bass and electric guitars, reggae bands also use **horn sections** that include trumpets, trombones and saxophones. The horn section might play riffs or help to emphasise the offbeat chords. These chords are usually played with an electronic **organ** sound. Some reggae bands also add extra percussion such as conga drums and tambourines.

WRITTEN ACTIVITIES

> REGGAE

1 Fill in the blanks

Write out and complete the text below, which contains basic facts about reggae music. Fill in the blanks with the words given below.

Reggae is music from _____ that developed in the _____. Reggae's musical influences include types of Caribbean music such as _____ and _____. Reggae always has _____ steady beats in each bar but the rhythms are often offbeat. The word for this is _____. The most famous reggae artist is _____ _____ who followed the religion _____.

FOUR   SYNCOPATION   JAMAICA   1960s
SKA   MENTO   BOB MARLEY   RASTAFARI

2 Reggae instruments

Listed below are five instruments that are used in reggae songs. Complete the table by adding the role that each instrument usually has in reggae music. Choose from the roles below (note that each instrument might have more than one role):

RHYTHM   CHORDS
RIFFS   BASS LINE

Instrument	Role in reggae music
Drum kit	
Bass guitar	
Saxophone	
Trumpet	
Organ	

3 Design a poster

In the 1970s Bob Marley played a series of gigs in London, including at the Rainbow Theatre (which is now a church) in Finsbury Park, north London. Design a poster for this concert – make it colourful, perhaps by using the colours associated with Bob and his religion: red, gold and green. Include some of Bob Marley's most famous song titles on the poster.

PRACTICAL ACTIVITIES

REGGAE

1 Reggae chord patterns

Reggae songs are built around simple chord patterns – some songs use just two or three chords. Practise playing a basic reggae riff on a keyboard using just C major. You can play the bass note with your left hand, or leave it out and just play the right-hand chords.

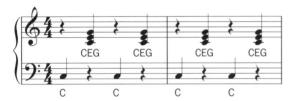

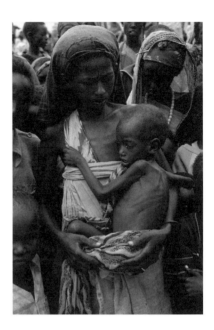

Now look at how this four-bar pattern uses C major, F major and G major chords:

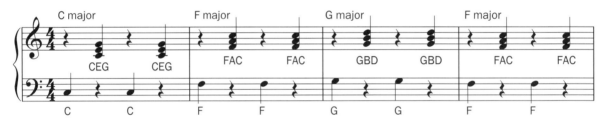

Next devise your own four-chord reggae riff. Make sure you get the offbeat feel by putting the chords on the second and fourth beats of the bar. If you can, add another layer – either a bass riff, which should have a completely different rhythm, or a melody on top. You may want to just use white-note chords to keep it simple.

2 Writing lyrics for a reggae song

Reggae songs traditionally deal with social justice issues such as equality between people. You can hear this in Bob Marley's famous song *One Love*:

> 'One love! One heart!
> Let's get together and feel all right.'

Write your own lyrics for a reggae song about a current issue you feel strongly about. The images on this page might help to inspire you.

Think about creating lyrics for a verse and a chorus. If you have time, try to develop a melody for them using the chord pattern you made up in the activity above.

Remember that reggae melodies are usually easy to sing. They often move from step to step and use much repetition.

MUSIC COVER LESSONS

TEACHER'S NOTES

EQUIPMENT REQUIRED

- Copies of the Factsheet to be handed out to students.
- Copies of the Written Activities worksheet to be handed out to students.
- Paper or exercise books to complete written work.
- Copies of the Practical Activities worksheet, if you feel confident in allowing students to undertake these tasks. The practical activities will require instruments (ideally keyboards or music ICT) for students to work on. Tuned percussion, guitars or the students' own instruments can also be used.
- An interactive whiteboard (optional). A PowerPoint presentation that accompanies this topic is available on the CD-ROM. This includes a reduction of the information on the factsheet and worksheets, accompanied by colour images. It also includes a link to the YouTube playlist for this topic (see below).

SUGGESTED LISTENING EXTRACTS

The following extracts are available in the YouTube playlist for this topic, which can be accessed from the PowerPoint presentation on the CD-ROM or from Rhinegold Education's YouTube channel.

- **Traditional African drumming**
- **Djembe example**
- **Mbira example**
- **Balafon example**
- **Kora example (Toumani Diabaté)**
- **Call and response singing by African children**
- **Paul Simon: 'Diamonds on the Soles of her Shoes'** from *Graceland*
- **David Fanshawe:** *African Sanctus*
- **'The Lion Sleeps Tonight' from** *The Lion King*

AFRICAN MUSIC

PRIOR KNOWLEDGE

This lesson does not require any previous study of African music. It can be set as an introductory or one-off lesson. You could see if students have studied African music at KS2, and may wish to use students' family links or personal experiences of Africa as a starting point.

It will be useful to remind students of the pentatonic (five note) scale. Some classes may have encountered this already in topics such as jazz, folk or Indonesian music. The notes of the scale are given on the Practical Activities worksheet.

SUGGESTED LESSON OUTLINE

A YouTube playlist is available that contains the suggested listening extracts listed to the left. It is not essential, but it would be useful to have extracts playing while the students are working.

A suggested starting activity would be to play an extract and ask the class to pool their knowledge and/or views on the musical style before giving out the Factsheet. The extracts in the playlist can be played in any order, but you may wish to start with the traditional drumming clip as students are likely to recognise this as being typically African. Students may even have played djembes themselves.

If a whole-class reading strategy is used, breaking this up with clips of the instruments will illustrate the information effectively, and the clip of the African children's singing may generate discussions and comments from students about the differences in school music-making between Africa and the West.

Fusion examples include the classical *African Sanctus* and the track from Paul Simon's *Graceland* album. The class can be encouraged to point out the African and Western features in these pieces.

The Factsheet contains all of the information needed to complete the activities. You may wish students to read through it individually,

TEACHER'S NOTES

ACTIVITY ANSWERS

Activity 1: fill in the blanks

a) The most common type of African drum is the **djembe**.

b) The mbira has metal keys and is often known as the **thumb** piano.

c) African music uses **polyrhythms** which are different rhythms played together.

d) 'The Lion Sleeps Tonight' was written by the South African **Solomon Linda**.

e) The **pentatonic** scale has five notes and is common in African and other types of world music.

f) Paul Simon's album **Graceland** (which was released in **1986**) fuses Western pop with African traditional music.

g) The balafon is a type of **xylophone** that uses **gourds** for resonators underneath the keys.

h) We call unaccompanied vocal music **a cappella**.

i) When a leader plays or sings one phrase, and this is answered by a group with a complementary phrase, this is known as **call** and **response**.

AFRICAN MUSIC

SUGGESTED LESSON OUTLINE (cont.)

or in pairs or small groups. The Activities worksheets can be given out with the Factsheet or afterwards. The activities can be undertaken in any order, and some students may wish to focus on a particular one or two.

If you feel confident with both the written and practical activities, you may wish to mix and match the activities within a lesson. The material can also be split across two lessons, with the first lesson focusing on going over the Factsheet and completing the written work, and the second lesson based on the practical activities.

Alternatively, completing two written tasks and starting off the practical work can fit within an hour-long lesson. The work could be completed in the next session if desired by the returning subject teacher (or the cover teacher if required).

Plenary activities can focus on key word terminology and awareness of style. Asking students to prepare three questions about the style and getting them to quiz each other is a simple follow-on activity, as is asking the class to list as many key words linked to the topic as possible without using their Factsheets.

If practical work is not an option, breaking up the written work with audio or visual clips of performances will ensure that the class receives a solid experience of the style.

FACTSHEET

AFRICAN MUSIC

INTRODUCTION

Africa is a vast continent with an enormous variety of landscapes, climates, languages and beliefs. African music is also very diverse, with many different styles of music ranging from traditional to popular. However, many of these share common features.

> **THE CURIOUS BEAUTY OF AFRICAN MUSIC IS THAT IT UPLIFTS EVEN AS IT TELLS A SAD TALE.**
>
> NELSON MANDELA

TRADITIONAL MUSIC

Traditional music serves a variety of purposes in the lives of African people. It is used at celebrations such as births, naming ceremonies, weddings and village feasts. It has historically played a part in tribal warfare and **rites of passage** too, and nowadays it is often a colourful part of the tourist industry across the continent. Traditional African music is nearly always taught in the **oral tradition**.

African dancers

Oral tradition: music learnt through listening and copying.

Rites of passage: ceremonies which mark moving to a new stage in life, such as when a child is considered to have become an adult.

AFRICAN INSTRUMENTS

Here are just some of the many varied instruments that can be found across Africa.

Djembe	This is the most common type of African drum and can produce a variety of sounds using different playing techniques.
Mbira	The mbira consists of metal keys attached to a wooden frame, and often plays interlocking **ostinatos** (patterns that are repeated over and over again). Bottle tops are often attached to the soundboard to create a buzzing sound.
Balafon	A type of large xylophone that has gourds hanging underneath the keys which act as resonators. Like the mbira, it usually plays repetitive ostinatos.
Kora	A west African instrument with a large gourd for a body, a long neck and strings that are plucked like a harp.
Talking drum	This has an hourglass shape and can produce a range of sounds that mimic speech.
Double bell	Double bells are used throughout Africa. They are metal bells with two heads, one low-pitched and one high-pitched. They often act as the timekeeper for an ensemble.

Djembe

Mbira

FACTSHEET

AFRICAN MUSIC

KEY WORDS

Polyrhythm	Different rhythms played together.
Call and response	A leader plays or sings one phrase (the 'call') and it is answered by a group with a complementary phrase (the 'response').
Oral tradition	Learning music by listening and copying rather than reading notation.
Pentatonic	A five-note scale common in many types of world music.
Heterophonic	A type of texture where different versions of the same melody are played together.
Syncopation	Offbeat rhythms – African music is full of syncopation.
Ostinato	A pattern that is repeated over and over.
A cappella	Unaccompanied vocal music.

AFRICAN FUSIONS

African music has had a huge influence on music around the world, from blues and jazz to reggae and calypso. Below are a couple of famous examples of music that fuses Western and African influences.

Graceland by Paul Simon

Released in 1986, this album fuses Western pop with South African music. It features songs by the choir Ladysmith Black Mambazo, who are famous for their style of singing known as **isicathymia**.

African Sanctus by David Fanshawe

This piece, written in 1972, fuses Western sacred choral music with recordings of traditional African music. The work is based on Fanshawe's own journey up the Nile River, during which he made the recordings that feature in this piece.

THE LION KING

This 1994 Disney film included hit songs by Elton John and Tim Rice. Lebo M, a South African composer, also worked on the film to give the score an African feel. He led the choir that features on the soundtrack, and can be heard singing the famous chant at the very start of the film.

One of the hits in *The Lion King* was the song 'The Lion Sleeps Tonight'. This was actually written in the 1920s by a South African called Solomon Linda, and was originally called 'Mbube' which is the Zulu word for 'lion'. The use of a catchy chant ('Wimoweh') and a soaring melody over the top have given the song a worldwide appeal.

GRIOTS

Griots play a very important role in West African music and have existed for thousands of years. They are highly respected performers who tend to specialise in one of three areas: speech (such as storytelling and poetry), song or instrumental music. The kora is the instrument most strongly associated with the griots, and in west Africa it is only members of a griot family who are traditionally allowed to play it. One of the most famous griots is the kora player Toumani Diabaté.

Lebo M & Elton John

MUSIC COVER LESSONS

WRITTEN ACTIVITIES

AFRICAN MUSIC

1 Fill in the blanks

Write out and complete the statements below using the information given on the Factsheet.

a) The most common type of African drum is the _____.

b) The mbira has metal keys and is often known as the _____ piano.

c) African music uses _____ which are different rhythms played together.

d) 'The Lion Sleeps Tonight' was written by the South African _____.

e) The _____ scale has five notes and is common in Africa and other types of world music.

f) Paul Simon's album _____ (which was released in _____) fuses Western pop with African traditional music.

g) The balafon is a type of _____ that uses _____ for resonators underneath the keys.

h) We call unaccompanied vocal music _____.

i) When a leader plays or sings one phrase, and this is answered by a group with a complementary phrase, this is known as _____ and _____.

2 Describing African music

You are asked to produce a pamphlet or poster giving information on African music for an International Culture Day being held at school. Using the information on the Factsheet, provide facts and illustrations and make sure that key words (and definitions) are used.

3 Fusion music

There are many examples of composers and musicians who have fused African music with other styles. Do you think musical fusion is a positive thing? Can it bring other benefits as well (not just musical ones)? Are there any disadvantages to fusion music? If possible, research the impact and effects of Paul Simon's *Graceland* album (mentioned on the Factsheet) to help you form your opinions.

Write down your views on fusion music, using examples to illustrate your points. Aim to produce a short essay – roughly one side of A4.

4 Social issues inspiring songwriting

Nelson Mandela says that African music 'uplifts even as it tells a sad tale'.

Africa is often portrayed by Western media in a negative light, with news features on famine, drought, political unrest and HIV. Write the lyrics for a song that presents a more positive picture of Africa, focusing on African music and dance. Think about the lively and joyful nature of much African music, and the richness and diversity of musical styles across the continent.

PRACTICAL ACTIVITIES

AFRICAN MUSIC

1 Using the pentatonic scale

The pentatonic scale is common in many world-music styles, including African music. Play through the scale below. Then try creating short phrases and ostinatos (repeated patterns) using the notes of this scale.

C D E G A

If you find it easier, you can use the black-note pentatonic scale, which is simply the five black notes on a piano (F# G# A# C# D#).

Once you have become confident at playing and improvising with this scale, use the picture below as a stimulus to devise a short improvisation or composition entitled *African Landscape*.

Decide on tempo and mood first. If you are using keyboards or ICT, choose sounds that will help to give your music an African feel, such as cowbells, drums, shakers, harp (if there is no kora sound) and xylophones.

2 Completing your song

Use the lyrics you came up with for Written Activity 4 as the basis for a whole song. Start by working out a simple chord pattern: this could just use the white-note chords of C major (C E G), F major (F A C) and G major (G B D). Practise playing your chord pattern in a lively rhythm.

Next work out a melody for your lyrics. Try to include some offbeat rhythms and to make the melody sound upbeat and joyful: this will reflect the positive lyrics of your song, and also help it to sound more African. You could read through Nelson Mandela's quote below to inspire you:

> **'The curious beauty of African music is that it uplifts even as it tells a sad tale. You may be poor, you may have only a ramshackle house, you may have lost your job, but that song gives you hope. African music is often about the aspirations of the African people, and it can ignite the political resolve of those who might otherwise be indifferent to politics.'**
>
> Nelson Mandela, *Long Walk To Freedom*

TEACHER'S NOTES

INDIAN MUSIC

EQUIPMENT REQUIRED

- Copies of the Factsheet to be handed out to students.
- Copies of the Written Activities worksheet to be handed out to students.
- Paper or exercise books to complete written work.
- Copies of the Practical Activities worksheet, if you feel confident in allowing students to undertake these tasks. The practical activities will require instruments (ideally keyboards or music ICT) for students to work on. Tuned percussion, guitars or the students' own instruments can also be used.
- An interactive whiteboard (optional). A PowerPoint presentation that accompanies this topic is available on the CD-ROM. This includes a reduction of the information on the factsheet and worksheets, accompanied by colour images. It also includes a link to the YouTube playlist for this topic (see below).

SUGGESTED LISTENING EXTRACTS

The following extracts are available in the YouTube playlist for this topic, which can be accessed from the PowerPoint presentation on the CD-ROM or from Rhinegold Education's YouTube channel.

- **Tabla example**
- **Sitar example (Ravi Shankar)**
- **Bansuri example**
- **Raga Desh performance**
- **George Harrison's sitar lesson**
- **Beatles: Within You Without You**
- **Bollywood song Wada Na Tod**

PRIOR KNOWLEDGE

The activities for this topic do not require any previous study of Indian music. However, many schools will have students who have knowledge or experience of India, its culture and possibly its musical styles. A useful starting point would be to ask the students to brainstorm their knowledge of India and Indian music, drawing on other subjects as well such as Geography and Religious Studies.

Bollywood films and music would also work well as an initial focus, leading to a discussion on the fusion of Indian classical music and Western pop. Simply playing one of the suggested extracts while students enter the room will alert them to the style: many students will recognise the distinctive sound of Indian music even if this is their first lesson on the topic.

SUGGESTED LESSON OUTLINE

A YouTube playlist is available that contains the suggested listening extracts listed to the left. It is not essential, but it would be useful to have extracts playing while the students are working.

A suggested starting activity would be to play an extract and ask the class to pool their knowledge and/or views on the musical style before giving out the Factsheet. The listening extracts can be used in any order but you may wish to start with a focus on instrumentation. The sitar and tabla are most commonly recognised by students. The brief clip of George Harrison's sitar lesson is a great example of learning in the oral tradition, and could be followed by the song *Within You Without You*, which highlights the Beatles' interest in Indian music.

The Factsheet contains all of the information needed to complete the tasks. You may wish students to read through it individually or in pairs or small groups. The Activities worksheets can be given out with the Factsheet or afterwards. The activities can be undertaken in any order, and some students may wish to focus on a particular one or two.

If you feel confident with both the practical and written activities, you may wish to mix and match the tasks within a lesson. The material can also be

TEACHER'S NOTES

INDIAN MUSIC

ACTIVITY ANSWERS

Activity 1: create a quiz on Indian music

a) What is the Indian film industry in Mumbai called?
   Bollywood

b) Name a famous sitar player.
   Ravi Shankar

c) How is Indian classical music learnt?
   Oral tradition

d) Name a bowed string instrument used in Indian classical music.
   Sarangi

e) Name a plucked string instrument used in Indian classical music.
   Sitar

f) Name a type of Indian drum.
   Tabla

g) Which instrument plays the drone?
   Tanpura

h) To which time of day is Raga Desh linked?
   Evening

i) Name the opening section of an instrumental performance.
   Alap

Activity 2: Indian versus Western classical music

Feature	Indian classical	Western classical
Scale	Raga	Major and minor
Rhythm	Tala	Time signature
Texture	Melody and drone	Melody and harmony
Bowed string	Sarangi	Violin
Plucked string	Sitar	Guitar

SUGGESTED LESSON OUTLINE (cont.)

split across two lessons, with the first lesson focusing on going over the Factsheet and completing the written work, and the second lesson based on the practical tasks.

Alternatively, completing two written tasks and starting off the practical work can fit within an hour-long lesson. The work could be completed in the next session if desired by the returning subject teacher (or the cover teacher if required).

Plenary activities can focus on key word terminology and awareness of style. Asking students to prepare three questions about the style and getting them to quiz each other is a simple follow-on activity, as is asking the class to list as many key words linked to the topic as possible without using their Factsheets.

If practical work is not an option, breaking up the written work with audio or visual clips of performances will ensure that the class receives a solid experience of the style.

FACTSHEET

INDIAN MUSIC

INTRODUCTION

The classical music of north India has developed over the last 2000 years and is closely linked to the Hindu religion. Its popularity in the West developed rapidly in the 1960s – partly thanks to the Beatles' interest in it – and it has had a major influence on composers of all sorts of music around the world.

> **INDIAN FOOD IS LIKE CLASSICAL MUSIC RAGA – IT TAKES TIME TO BUILD UP TO A CRESCENDO.**
>
> SHOBHAA DÉ

THE THREE COMPONENTS OF INDIAN CLASSICAL MUSIC

- **Melody**: this uses the notes of the **raga**. Melodies in Indian classical music can be played by instruments such as the **sitar** or **sarangi**. It is the most important aspect of Indian classical music.
- **Drone**: Indian classical music doesn't have chords or harmony but instead uses a drone: sustained notes that provide a constant accompaniment, usually played by the **tanpura**.
- **Rhythm**: this is provided by the **tabla**, which plays rhythmic patterns based on the **tala**.

HOW IS INDIAN MUSIC TAUGHT?

Indian classical music is not written down in Western notation but is taught through listening and playing by ear. Traditionally a pupil will live with a master performer and learn to play through imitation. The term for this is **oral tradition**.

RAGA

In simple terms, a raga (or rag) is an Indian scale. In a piece of Indian classical music, a performer will improvise around the notes of this scale, initially playing short phrases but then developing more complex melodies. There are different types of raga, and the notes may change between the ascending and descending versions of the scale. One example is Raga Desh, which has B in the ascent and B♭ in the descent:

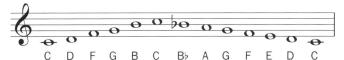

C D F G B C B♭ A G F E D C

Another important feature of raga is that each one is linked to a particular time of day or season. Raga Desh, for example, is a late evening raga associated with the monsoon season.

TALA

A tala (or tal) is a rhythmic cycle: a fixed pattern of beats that is repeated continuously throughout a piece. In the same way that the raga provides the melodic framework for a piece, the tala provides the rhythmic framework. The tabla player will use the tala to decide what rhythms to play. One of the most common tala is Tintal: a 16-beat cycle that is divided into four sections of four beats each.

STRUCTURE OF A PERFORMANCE

The following structure is often used for an instrumental performance of Indian classical music:

Alap	A slow, improvised opening section. The notes of the raga are introduced and explored freely by the melody instrument, with just a drone accompanying (but no tabla).
Jor	The soloist continues to improvise around the raga but with more of a steady pulse.
Jhala	This section is still improvised but the rhythms become faster and more complex. The music is more **virtuosic** (technically demanding).
Gat	Here the soloist stops improvising and instead performs a pre-composed/fixed passage of music. The tabla also enters, playing the chosen tala.

FACTSHEET

INDIAN MUSIC

INDIAN CLASSICAL INSTRUMENTS

- **Sitar:** a plucked string instrument with a very long neck, used to play the melody. An important feature of this instrument are the extra 'sympathetic' strings, which resonate by themselves when the main strings are played, creating a distinctive shimmering sound (sometimes described as 'twangy').
- **Tanpura:** similar to the sitar but with fewer strings and no frets. It is used to play the drone.
- **Tabla:** two small drums that can produce a huge variety of sounds by using different handstrokes.
- **Harmonium:** a box-shaped keyboard instrument that has hand-operated bellows at the back.
- **Sarangi:** a bowed string instrument that is a little like the violin, although played while sitting cross-legged with the instrument held upright against the chest.
- **Bansuri:** a bamboo flute.

Tanpura

Tabla

Harmonium

Sarangi

George Harrison and Ravi Shankar

THE BEATLES IN INDIA

George Harrison, the lead guitarist of The Beatles, visited India in 1966 where he studied Indian music with the great sitar player Ravi Shankar. He returned in 1968 with the rest of the band to practise meditation. Several Beatles' songs display an Indian influence as a result, such as *Within You Without You* and *The Inner Light*.

BOLLYWOOD FILM MUSIC

'Bollywood' refers to the film industry that is based in the Indian city of Mumbai, which is one of the largest film industries in the world. Bollywood films often mix comedy, drama, romance and action, and most of them are musicals. In fact the songs – which tend to fuse Indian classical influences with Western pop – can make or break a film.

WRITTEN ACTIVITIES

INDIAN MUSIC

1 Create a quiz on Indian music

Below are nine terms related to Indian music. Each is the answer to a question, but the questions have been mixed up. Can you create the correct version of the quiz using the information on the Factsheet? Write each question out followed by the correct answer.

Answer	Question
Tanpura	What is the Indian film industry in Mumbai called?
Tabla	Name a famous sitar player.
Bollywood	How is Indian classical music learnt?
Sitar	Name a bowed string instrument used in Indian classical music.
Sarangi	Name a plucked string instrument used in Indian classical music.
Oral tradition	Name a type of Indian drum.
Evening	Which instrument plays the drone?
Alap	To which time of day is Raga Desh linked?
Ravi Shankar	Name the opening section of an instrumental performance.

2 Indian versus Western classical music

This table shows some of the differences and similarities between Indian and Western classical music. Fill in the gaps (some details have been completed for you).

Feature	Indian classical	Western classical
Scale		Major and minor
Rhythm		Time signature
Texture		Melody and harmony
Bowed string		Violin
Plucked string		Guitar

3 About Indian music

Using the details provided on the Factsheet, create an illustrated spider diagram to give information about Indian music to someone who has never heard it before. Below are some words to start you off.

TABLA   RAVI SHANKAR

TALA   RAGA

INDIAN MUSIC

PRACTICAL ACTIVITIES

INDIAN MUSIC

1 Improvising using Raga Vibhas

Play through the notes of Raga Vibhas on either a keyboard or another pitched instrument. The notes are:

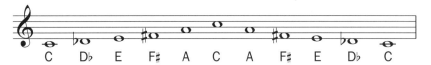

Now try making up short patterns and melodies that use these notes. In an Indian classical performance, melodies often start out slowly and simply by just using a few notes of the raga, but grow in complexity and speed until all the notes of the raga are being used. Can you take this approach with your improvisation?

Once you are confident with the notes of the raga, you could add a drone in the lower part of the keyboard by holding down the notes A and C (use a 'string' sound or something else that will sustain). Alternatively, you could alternate the notes A and C as below:

2 Composing a morning piece

Raga Vibhas is a morning raga. Using Raga Vibhas (the notes are given above) and an accompanying drone, create a short piece inspired by the idea of sunrise.

If possible, start by recording a drone track that just repeats the notes A and C over and over again in a chosen pattern. Then use the notes of the raga to create a melody on top.

The melody could start out slowly in a free rhythm and then become busier as the sun rises.

If you have time, you could add a tala to your piece by creating a rhythmic pattern that lasts for 16 beats. Like the drone, this should be repeated constantly beneath the melody.

The Taj Mahal at sunrise